KU-444-333

SPANISH TRAVELMATE

compiled by
LEXUS
with
Alicia de Benito de Harland
and
Mike Harland

RICHARD DREW PUBLISHING
Glasgow

RICHARD DREW PUBLISHING LTD.
6 CLAIRMONT GARDENS
GLASGOW G3 7LW
SCOTLAND

First Published 1982
First Reprint April 1982
Second Reprint May 1984
Third Reprint May 1985
New Edition 1986

ISBN 0 904002 75 6

Printed and bound in Great Britain by
Cox & Wyman Ltd.

YOUR TRAVELMATE
gives you one single easy-to-use list of useful
words and phrases to help you communicate in
Spanish.

Built into this list are:
– Travel Tips with facts and figures which provide
valuable information
– Spanish words you'll see on signs and notices
– typical replies to some of the things you might
want to say.

There is a menu reader on pages 70–71 and
numbers and the Spanish alphabet are given on
pages 127–128.

Your TRAVELMATE also tells you how to
pronounce Spanish. Just read the pronunciations
as though they were English and you will
communicate – although you might not sound like
a native speaker.

One special sound:
h is like the ch in Scottish 'loch'

If no pronunciation is given then the word itself
can be spoken as though it were English. And
sometimes only part of a word or phrase needs a
pronunciation guide. Vowels in italics show
which part of a word to stress.

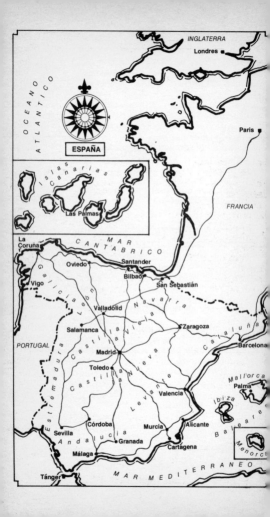

a, an un; una [oon, *oo*na]
   70 pesetas a litre setenta pesetas el litro
abdomen el abdomen [abd*oh*-men]
abierto *open*
aboard a bordo
about: is he about? ¿está por aquí? [. . . ak*ee*]
   about 15 unos quince [*oo*noss k*ee*ntheh]
   about 2 o'clock sobre las dos [s*oh*-breh]
above por encima [por ent*h*eema]
   above that por encima de eso
abroad en el extranjero [estran*h*eh-roh]
absolutely! ¡desde luego! [d*e*zdeh lweh-goh]
accelerator el acelerador [atheh-lerad*o*r]
accept aceptar [athept*a*r]
accident un accidente [aktheed*e*nteh]
   there's been an accident ha habido un
   accidente [ah ab*ee*doh oon . . .]
» *TRAVEL TIP: no reciprocal health agreements;*
   often quickest to stop a vehicle and find the
   nearest Red Cross (Cruz Roja) point or hospital
accommodation alojamiento [aloh*am*-yentoh]
   we need accommodation for three
   necesitamos alojamiento para tres personas
   [nethesseet*ah*-moss . . .]
» *TRAVEL TIP: apart from hotels there are also three*
   categories of 'pensión' (boarding house) often
   cheaper and quite adequate with meals
   available
accurate exacto [eggs-*a*ktoh]
ache un dolor
   it aches me duele [meh dweh-leh]

across al otro lado
  how do we get across? ¿cómo se cruza?
  [. . . krootha]
  across the street al otro lado de la calle
  [. . . ka-yeh]
adaptor un adaptador
address la dirección [deerekth-yon]
  will you give me your address? ¿me quiere
  dar su dirección? [meh kee-eh-reh . . .]
admission la entrada
advance: can we book in advance? ¿se
  pueden hacer las reservas por adelantado? [seh
  pweh-den ath-air . . .]
advert un anuncio [anoon-thee-oh]
afraid: I'm afraid I don't know me temo que
  no lo sé [meh teh-moh keh noh loh seh]
  I'm afraid so me temo que sí
  I'm afraid not me temo que no
after: after you usted primero [oosteh . . .]
  after 2 o'clock después de las dos [dess-pwess]
afternoon la tarde [tar-deh]
  in the afternoon por la tarde
  good afternoon buenas tardes [bweh-nass
  tardess]
  this afternoon esta tarde
aftershave 'aftershave'
again otra vez [oh-tra veth]
against contra
age edad [eh-da]
  under age menor de edad
  it takes ages se tarda mucho [moochoh]
ago: a week ago hace una semana [ah-theh
  oona seh-mah-na]
  it wasn't long ago no hace mucho tiempo [noh
  ah-theh moochoh tee-empoh]
  how long ago was that? ¿cuánto tiempo hace
  de eso? [kwantoh . . . ah-theh . . .]
agree: I agree estoy de acuerdo [. . . akwair-
  doh]; **it doesn't agree with me** no me sienta
  bien [noh meh see-enta bee-en]

agua potable *drinking water*
air aire [eye-reh]
 by air en avión [av-yon]
 by airmail por avión
 with air-conditioning con aire acondicionado
 [–deeth-yonah-doh]
airport el aeropuerto [ah-airoh-pwair-toh]
alarm la alarma
 alarm clock un despertador
alcohol alcohol [alko-ol]
 is it alcoholic? ¿tiene alcohol? [tee-eh-neh . . .]
alive vivo [vee–]
 is he still alive? ¿vive todavía? [vee-veh
 toh-davee-ah]
all todo [toh-doh]
 all night toda la noche [toh-da la notcheh]
 that's all wrong está todo mal
 all right de acuerdo [deh akwair-doh]
 I'm all right estoy bien [. . . bee-en]
 that's all eso es todo
 thank you – not at all gracias – de nada
 [grath-yass-deh nah-da]
allergic alérgico [alair-heekoh]
 I'm allergic to . . . soy alérgico a . . .
allowed permitido
 is it allowed? ¿está permitido?
 allow me permítame [pair-meeta-meh]
almost casi [kah-see]
alone solo
 did you come here alone? ¿ha venido solo?
 [ah . . .]
 leave me alone déjeme en paz [dehemeh em
 path]
alquiler de coches *car hire*
already ya
also también [tamb-yen]
alternator un alternador [al-tair-nador]
although aunque [owng-keh]
alto *halt*
altogether del todo

....

what does that make altogether? ¿cuánto es
en total? [kwantoh . . .]

always siempre [see-em-preh]

a.m. de la mañana [. . . man-yah-na] *(in
conversation). In timetables the 24-hour system
is used.*

ambassador el embajador [emba-hador]

ambulance una ambulancia [amboolanthee-a]
get an ambulance! ¡llame a una ambulancia!
[yah-meh . . .]

» *TRAVEL TIP: few available: might be advisable to
use a car and race to hospital waving a white
handkerchief out of window and blaring horn*

America América

American americano

among entre [entreh]

amps amperios [ampeh-ree-oss]
15-amp fuse un fusible de quince amperios
[foo-see-bleh deh keentheh . . .]

anchor el ancla

and y [ee]

andén platform

angry enfadado
I'm very angry about it estoy muy [mwee]
enfadado por ello [eh-yoh]
please don't get angry haga [ah-ga] el favor
de no enfadarse [emfadar-seh]

animal un animal

ankle el tobillo [toh-bee-yoh]

anniversary: it's our anniversary es nuestro
aniversario [. . . nwess-troh . . .]

annoy: he's annoying me me está molestando
[meh . . .]
it's very annoying es muy molesto [mwee]

anorak un anorak

another: can we have another room? ¿puede
darnos otra habitación? [pweh-deh . . .
abbeetath-yon]
another beer, please por favor, otra cerveza
[. . . thair-veh-tha]

answer: what was his answer? ¿qué
respondió? [keh respond-yoh]
there was no answer no hubo respuesta
[. . . *oo*boh ress-pw*ess*-ta]
antifreeze anticongelante [anti-kon*h*ellanteh]
**any: have you got any bananas/
butter?** ¿tiene usted plátanos/mantequilla?
[tee-*eh*-neh oost*eh* . . . manteh-k*ee*ya]
I haven't got any no tengo
anybody cualquiera [kwal-kee-*eh*-ra]
can anybody help? ¿alguien puede ayudar?
[*a*l-ghee-en pw*eh*-deh ah-yoo-d*a*r]
anything algo
I don't want anything no quiero nada
[. . . kee-*eh*-roh . . .]
aparcamiento car park
aperitif un aperitivo [–tee–]
apology una disculpa
please accept my apologies por favor, acepte
mis disculpas [. . . ath*e*pteh meess . . .]
I want an apology quiero que me pida
disculpas [kee-*eh*-roh keh meh p*ee*da . . .]
appendicitis apendicitis [–th*ee*-teess]
appetite apetito [–tee–]
I've lost my appetite he perdido el apetito [eh
pair-d*ee*doh el apeh-t*ee*-toh]
apple una manzana [man-th*ah*-na]
application form un impreso de solicitud
[. . . eempreh-soh deh soleetheet*oo*]
appointment una cita [th*ee*–]
can I make an appointment?
(with doctor) quería pedir hora
[ker*ee*-a ped*ee*r *o*ra]
apricot un albaricoque [albareek*o*keh]
April abril [abr*ee*l]
aqualung botellas de oxígeno [bot-*eh*-yass deh
ox-*ee*-*h*ennoh]
archaeology arqueología [arkeh-ollo-*hee*-a]
area la zona [th*o*na]
arm el brazo [–th–]

....

around *see* **about**

arrange: will you arrange it? ¿lo arreglará usted? [. . . oost*eh*]

it's all arranged todo está arregl*a*do

arrest *(verb)* detener [deh-ten*air*]

he's been arrested le han detenido [leh an deh-ten*ee*doh]

arrival la llegada [yeh-g*a*h-da]

arrive llegar [yeh-g*a*r]

we only arrived yesterday llegamos tan sólo ayer [yeh-g*a*h-moss . . . ah-y*ai*r]

art el arte [–teh]

art gallery museo de bellas artes [moo-s*eh*-oh deh b*eh*-yass *a*rtess]

arthritis artritis [ar-tr*ee*-teess]

artificial artificial [arteefeeth-y*a*l]

artist un pintor [peen-t*o*r]

as: as quickly as you can lo más de prisa que pueda [loh mass deh pr*ee*-sa keh pweh-da]

as much as you can tanto como pueda [. . . pw*eh*-da]

do as I do haga como yo [*a*h-ga . . .]

as you like como usted quiera [. . . oost*eh* kee-*eh*-ra]

ascensor lift

aseos toilets

ashore: to go ashore desembarc*a*r

ashtray un cenicero [thenee-th*eh*-roh]

ask pregunt*a*r

I didn't ask for that no había pedido eso [no ab*ee*-a ped*ee*doh *eh*-soh]

could you ask him to . . .? ¿podría pedirle que . . .? [pod-r*ee*-a ped*ee*r-leh keh]

asleep: he's still asleep todavía está durmiendo [todav*ee*-a esta door-mee-*e*n-doh]

asparagus un espárrago

aspirin una aspirina [asspeer*ee*na]

assistant un ayudante [ah-yoo-d*a*nteh]
(shop-) un dependiente [–dee-*e*nteh]

asthma asma [*a*zma]

at: at the cafe en el café
  at my hotel en mi hotel [... mee oh-tell]
atención al tren beware of trains
atmosphere la atmósfera [atmoss-feh-ra]
attitude una actitud [akteetoo]
attractive guapa [gwah-pa]
  I think you're very attractive me pareces
  muy guapa [meh pareh-thess mwee gwah-pa]
aubergine una berenjena [berren-heh-na]
August agosto [agoss-toh]
aunt: my aunt mi tía [mee tee-a]
Australia Australia [ows-trah-lee-a]
Australian australiano [-yah-noh]
authorities las autoridades [ow-torree-dah-
  dess]
automatic *(car)* automático [owtoh–]
autopista motorway
autoservicio self-service
autumn otoño [oh-tohn-yoh]
  in the autumn en otoño
away: is it far away from here? ¿está muy
  lejos de aquí? [... mwee leh-hoss deh akee]
  go away! ¡lárguese! [largheh-seh]
awful terrible [terree-bleh]
axle el eje [eh-heh]
baby un bebé [beh-beh]
  we'd like a baby-sitter quisiéramos una
  baby-sitter [keess-yeh-ramoss ...]
back: I've got a bad back padezco de dolor de
  espalda [padeth-koh ...]
  I'll be back soon estaré de vuelta pronto
  [esstareh deh vwelta ...]
  can I have my money back? ¿me puede
  devolver el importe? [meh pweh-deh deh-
  volvair ... –teh]
  come back! ¡vuelva! [vwelva]
  I go back tomorrow me vuelvo mañana
  [meh ...]
  at the back por detrás
bacon bacon

....

bacon and eggs huevos con bacon [weh-voss . . .]

bad malo; **it's not bad** no está mal

too bad! ¡qué le vamos a hacer! [keh leh vah-moss athair]

bag una bolsa

(handbag, suitcase) un bolso

baggage equipaje [eckee-p*a*h-*h*eh]

baker's la panadería [–*ee*-a]

balcony un balcón

a room with a balcony una habitación con balcón [abbee-tath-y*o*n . . .]

ball una pelota

ball-point pen un bol*í*grafo

banana un pl*á*tano

band *(mus)* la orquesta [ork*e*ssta]

bandage una venda

could you change the bandage? ¿quiere cambiar el vendaje? [kee-*e*h-reh kambee-*a*r el vend*a*h-*h*eh]

bank el banco; *(of river)* la orilla [or*ee*-ya]

» *TRAVEL TIP: banking hours: 9–1 Mon-Sat; see* **public holidays, change**

bar el bar

when does the bar open? ¿a qué hora se abre el bar? [ah keh *o*ra seh *a*h-breh . . .]

» *TRAVEL TIP: see* **café**

barber's una peluquer*í*a de caballeros [pelookeh-r*ee*-a deh kaba-yeh-ross]

bargain: it's a real bargain es una verdadera ganga [. . . vairda-d*e*h-ra . . .]

barmaid la camarera [–r*e*h-ra]

barman el camarero [–r*e*h-roh]

basket un cesto [th–]

bath un baño [b*a*hn-yoh]

can I have a bath? ¿puedo darme un baño? [pw*e*h-doh d*a*r-meh oon . . .]

could you give me a bath towel? ¿me podría dar una toalla de baño? [meh podr*ee*-a dar oona toh-*a*h-ya deh . . .]

bathing el baño [bahn-yoh]
  bathing costume traje de baño [trah-heh deh . . .]
bathroom cuarto de baño [kwartoh deh bahn-yoh]
  we want a room with a private bathroom queremos una habitación con cuarto de baño [keh-reh-moss oona abbee-tath-yon kon . . .]
  can I use your bathroom? ¿puedo usar su cuarto de baño? [pweh-doh oosar soo . . .]
battery la batería [bateh-ree-a]
be ser [sair]
  be good sé bueno [seh bweh-noh]
  don't be lazy no seas vago [. . . seh-ass vah-goh]
beach la playa [pla-ya]
  on the beach en la playa
beans judías [hoodee-ass]
  runner beans judías verdes [. . . vair-dess]
  dried beans judías blancas
  broad beans habas [ah-bass]
beautiful precioso [preth-yoh-soh]
  that was a beautiful meal ha sido una comida estupenda [ah see-doh oona kommeeda esstoopenda]
because porque [por-keh]
  because of the bad weather debido al mal tiempo [debeedoh . . . tee-empoh]
bed una cama
  single bed/double bed cama individual/ cama doble [. . . doh-bleh]
  you haven't changed my bed no me ha cambiado las sábanas [noh meh ah kambee-ah-doh . . .]
  bed and breakfast alojamiento y desayuno [alo-ham-yentoh ee dessa-yoonoh]
  I want to go to bed quiero acostarme [kee-eh-roh . . .–meh]
bedroom un dormitorio

bee una abeja [abeh-*h*a]

beef carne de vaca [k*a*rneh . . .]

beer cerveza [thairveh-tha]
two beers, please dos cervezas, por favor
» *TRAVEL TIP: cerveza implies lager; nearest
equivalent to British beer is 'cerveza negra'*

before: before breakfast antes de desayunar
[*a*n-tess deh dessa-yoo-n*a*r]
before we leave antes de march*a*rnos
I haven't been here before nunca había
estado aquí [noonka ab*ee*-a esst*a*h-doh ak*ee*]

begin: when does it begin? ¿cuándo empieza?
[kw*a*ndoh empee-*e*h-tha]

beginner principiante [preen-theep-y*a*nteh]

behind detrás
the car behind me el coche de detrás de mí
[. . .k*o*tcheh . . .]

believe: I don't believe you no le creo [noh leh
kr*e*h-oh]; **I believe you** le creo

bell *(in hotel etc)* el timbre [t*ee*m-breh]

belong: that belongs to me eso es mío
who does this belong to? ¿de quién es esto?
[deh kee-*e*n ess *e*sstoh]

below abajo [ab*a*h-*h*oh]

belt un cinturón [theen–]

bend *(in road)* una curva [k*oo*rva]

berries bayas [b*a*-yass]

berth *(on ship)* una litera [leet-*e*h-ra]

beside junto a [*h*oontoh ah]

best el mejor [m*e*hor]
it's the best holiday I've ever had son las
mejores vacaciones de mi vida [. . . m*e*horess
vakath-yoness deh mee v*ee*da]

better mejor [m*e*hor]
haven't you got anything better? ¿no tiene
nada mejor? [noh tee-*e*h-neh . . .]
are you feeling better? ¿se siente usted
mejor? [seh see-*e*nteh oost*e*h . . .]
I'm feeling a lot better me siento mucho
mejor

between entre [entreh]
beyond más allá [mass a-ya]
  beyond the mountains más allá de las
  montañas [. . . montahn-yass]
bicycle una bicicleta [beethee-kleh-ta]
  can we hire bicycles here? ¿se pueden
  alquilar bicicletas aquí? [seh pweh-den alkeelar
  . . . akee]
bienvenido welcome
big grande [–deh]
  a big one uno grande
  that's too big eso es demasiado grande [. . .
  demass-yah-doh . . .]
  it's not big enough no es suficientemente
  grande [. . . soofeeth-yenteh-menteh . . .]
  have you got a bigger one? ¿tiene usted otro
  más grande? [tee-eh-neh oosteh . . .]
bikini un bikini
bill la cuenta [kwenta]
  could I have the bill, please? la cuenta, por
  favor
binding *(ski)* atadura [–doora]
bird un pájaro [pa-haroh]
birthday cumpleaños [koompleh-an-yoss]
  it's my birthday es mi cumpleaños [ess
  mee . . .]
  happy birthday! ¡feliz cumpleaños!
  [feleeth . . .]
bit: just a little bit sólo un poquito [. . . poh-
  kee-toh]
  that's a bit too expensive es un poco caro
  a big bit un pedazo grande [pedah-thoh
  grandeh]
  a bit of that cake un pedazo de esa tarta
bite una picadura
  I've been bitten *(insect)* me ha picado un bicho
  [meh ah peekah-doh oon beechoh] *(dog)* me ha
  mordido un perro [. . . ah mordeedoh . . .]
bitter *(taste)* amargo
black negro

....

he's had a blackout ha sufrido un desmayo
[ah soof*ree*doh oon dess-m*a*-yoh]
bland suave [sw*ah*-veh]
blanket una manta
  I'd like another blanket ¿me da otra manta,
por favor?
bleach lejía [le*hee*-a]
bleed sangrar
  he's bleeding está sangrando
bless you! *(after sneeze)* ¡Jesús! [*h*eh-s*ooss*]
blind ciego [th*ee*-*e*h-goh]
  blind spot *(driving)* punto ciego [p*oo*ntoh . . .]
blister una ampolla [amp*oh*-ya]
blocked *(pipe)* atascada *(road)* cortada
blonde una rubia [r*oo*b-ya]
blood sangre [s*a*ngreh]
  his blood group is . . . su grupo sanguíneo
es . . . [soo gr*oo*poh sang-gh*ee*n-*e*h-oh]
  I've got high blood pressure tengo la tensión
alta [. . . tenss-yon . . .]
  he needs a blood transfusion necesita una
transfusión [nethess*ee*ta oona transfooss-yon]
bloody mary vodka con zumo de tomate
[. . . th*oo*moh deh tom*ah*-teh]
blouse una blusa [bl*oo*-sa]
blue azul [ath*oo*l]
board: full board pensión completa [penss-yon
kompl*e*h-ta]
  half board media pensión [m*ai*d-ya . . .]
  boarding pass tarjeta de embarque [tarh*e*h-
ta de emb*a*rkeh]
boat un barco
body el cuerpo [kw*ai*rpoh]
  dead body un cad*á*ver [–vair]
boil hervir; *(medical)* un forúnculo
  do we have to boil the water? ¿es necesario
hervir el agua? [. . . nethess*a*r-yoh airv*ee*r el
*a*hg-wa]
  boiled egg un huevo pasado por agua [oon
w*e*h-voh . . . *a*hg-wa]

bone hueso [weh-soh]

bonnet *(car)* el capó

book un libro [lee–]

    booking office el despacho de billetes [. . . deh bee-yeh-tess]

    can I book a seat for . . .? deseo reservar un asiento para . . . [deh-seh-oh reh-sairvar oon ass-yentoh . . .]

    I'd like to book a table for two quisiera reservar una mesa para dos personas [keess-yeh-ra . . .]

    bookshop una librería [leebreh-ree-a]

boot una bota

    (car) el portaequipajes [porta-eckee-pahess]

booze bebida [bebeeda]

    I had too much booze last night bebí demasiado anoche [bebee demass-yah-doh anotcheh]

border la frontera

bored: I'm bored estoy aburrido [. . . aboorreedoh]

boring aburrido [aboorreedoh]

born: I was born in . . . nací en . . . [nathee . . .]

borrow: can I borrow . . .? ¿puede prestarme . . .? [pweh-deh . . .–meh]

boss el jefe [heh-feh]

both los dos

    I'll take both of them me llevo los dos [meh yeh-voh loss doss]

bottle una botella [boteh-ya]

    bottle-opener un abrebotellas [ah-breh–]

bottom: at the bottom of the hill al fondo de la cuesta [. . . kwessta]

bowels el vientre [vee-entreh]

bowl *(basin)* una palangana

box una caja [kah-ha]

boy un chico [cheekoh]

boyfriend: my boyfriend mi amigo [mee ameegoh]

bra un sostén

bracelet una pulsera [poolseh-ra]

brake *(noun)* el freno [freh-noh]
  could you check the brakes? ¿quiere
  revisarme los frenos? [kee-eh-reh reh-
  veesarmeh loss freh-noss]
  I had to brake suddenly tuve que frenar
  bruscamente [tooveh keh freh-nar
  brooskamenteh]
  he didn't brake no frenó

brandy coñac [kon-yak]

bread pan
  could we have some bread and butter?
  ¿nos pone un poco de pan con mantequilla?
  [. . . poh-neh . . . manteh-kee-ya]
  some more bread, please más pan, por favor

break *(verb)* romper [romp-air]
  I think I've broken my arm me parece que
  me he roto el brazo [meh pareh-theh keh meh eh
  rotoh el brah-thoh]

breakable frágil [frah-heel]

breakdown una avería [aveh-ree-a]
  I've had a breakdown he tenido una avería
  [eh tenee-doh . . .]
  nervous breakdown una crisis nerviosa
  [kreeseess nairvee-osa]
  » *TRAVEL TIP: breakdown services: nearest garage!*

breakfast el desayuno [dessa-yoonoh]
  English/continental breakfast desayuno
  anglosajón/continental [. . . anglosahon]
  » *TRAVEL TIP: try typical 'chocolate con churros',*
  fritters dunked in hot chocolate

breast el pecho

breath aliento [al-yentoh]
  he's getting very short of breath se está
  quedando sin resuello [seh esta keh-dandoh
  seen reh-swell-yoh]

breathe respirar [resspeerar]
  I can't breathe no puedo respirar [noh
  pweh-doh . . .]

bridge un puente [pw*e*nteh]

briefcase la cartera [kart*e*h-ra]

brighten up: do you think it'll brighten up later? ¿cree usted que se despejará? [kr*e*h-eh . . . keh seh desspeh-*h*ara]

brilliant brillante [bree-y*a*nteh]

bring traer [trah-*a*ir]
could you bring it to my hotel? ¿podría traérmelo a mi hotel? [podr*ee*-a trah-*a*ir-meh-loh ah mee oh-t*e*l]

Britain Gran Bretaña [. . . bret*a*hn-ya]

British británico

brochure un foll*e*to
have you got any brochures about . . .? ¿tiene usted algún folleto sobre . . .? [tee-*e*h-neh oost*e*h algo*o*n foy*e*h-toh s*o*h-breh]

broken roto
you've broken it lo ha roto usted [loh ah r*o*h-toh oost*e*h]
it's broken está roto
my room/car has been broken into me han desvalijado la habitación/han penetrado en mi coche [meh an dess-valee-*h*ah-doh la abbeh-tath-yon/an . . . mee k*o*tcheh]

brooch un broche [–eh]

brother: my brother mi hermano [mee air-m*a*h-noh]

brown marrón; *(tanned)* moreno [mor*e*h-noh]
brown paper papel de embal*a*r

browse: can I just browse around? ¿puedo echar una ojeada? [pw*e*h-doh . . . oh-*h*eh-*a*h-da]

bruise un carden*a*l

brunette *(noun)* una morena [mor*e*h-na]

brush *(noun)* un cepillo [thep*e*e-yoh]
(artist's) un pincel [–th*e*l]

Brussels sprouts coles de Bruselas [k*o*h-less deh broo-s*e*h-lass]

bucket un cubo [k*oo*boh]

buffet un buff*e*t; *(on a train)* vagón restaurante [. . . rest-ow-r*a*nteh]

....

building un edificio [–feeth-yoh]

bulb una bombilla [–beeya]
  the bulb's gone se ha fundido la bombilla [seh ah foondeedoh . . .]

bull el toro
  a bull fight una corrida de toros [korree-da deh . . .]

bump: he's had a bump on the head se ha dado un golpe en la cabeza [seh ah dah-doh oon golpeh en la kabeh-tha]

bumper el parachoques [–choh-kess]

bunch of flowers un ramo de flores [–floress]

bunk una litera [leeteh-ra]
  bunk beds literas

buoy una boya

burglar un ladrón
  they've taken all my money se han llevado todo mi dinero [seh an yeh-vah-doh toh-doh mee deeneh-roh]

burnt: this meat is burnt esta carne está quemada [. . . karneh . . . keh-mah-da]
  my arms are burnt me he quemado los brazos [meh eh keh-mah-doh loss brah-thoss]
  can you give me something for these burns? ¿puede darme algo para estas quemaduras? [pweh-deh darmeh . . . keh-madoorass]

bus un autobús [ow-toh-booss]
  bus stop la parada del autobús
  could you tell me when we get there? ¿hará el favor de avisarme cuando lleguemos allí? [ara el favor deh aveesarmeh kwandoh yeh-gheh-moss a-yee]

business un negocio [negoth-yoh]
  I'm here on business estoy aquí de negocios [. . . akee . . .]
  business trip viaje de negocios [vee-ah-heh deh negoth-yoss]
  none of your business! ¡no es asunto suyo! [noh ess assoontoh soo-yoh]

....

bust el pecho
» *TRAVEL TIP: bust measurements*

UK	32	34	36	38	40
Spain	80	87	91	97	102

busy ocupado [–koo–]
(*telephone*) comunicando [–moo–]
  are you busy? ¿está usted ocupado?
  [. . . oost*eh* . . .]
but pero [peh-roh]
  not . . . but . . . no . . . sino . . . [seenoh]
butcher's la carnicería [karneeth*eh*-ree-a]
butter mantequilla [mantek*ee*ya]
button un bot*ó*n
buy: I'll buy it lo compro
by: I'm here by myself he venido solo [eh
  ven*ee*doh . . .]
  are you by yourself? ¿está usted solo? [est*a*
  oost*eh* . . .]
  can you do it by tomorrow? ¿puede tenerlo
  hecho para mañana? [pw*eh*-deh ten*ai*rloh
  *e*tchoh . . .]
  by train/car/plane en tren/coche/avión
  I parked by the trees aparqué junto a los
  árboles [apark*eh* h*oo*ntoh ah loss *a*rboless]
  who's it made by? ¿quién lo fabrica? [kee-*e*n
  loh fabr*ee*ka]
caballeros gentlemen
cabaret un cabaret [oon kabar*eh*]
cabbage una col
cabin (*on ship*) un camarote [kamaroh-teh]
cable (*in car etc*) un cable [k*a*h-bleh]
café una cafetería [kafeh-teh-ree-a]
» *TRAVEL TIP: cafetería/café/bar all roughly
  equivalent: all sell non-alcoholic and alcoholic
  drinks and snacks; open all day; children
  welcome; cheaper to eat or drink at the bar*
caja cash desk
cake un past*e*l
  a piece of cake un pedazo de tarta [peh-
  d*a*h-thoh . . .]

calculator una calculadora
caliente hot
call: will you call the manager? ¿quiere
llamar al director? [kee-*eh*-reh yam*a*r al
deerek*to*r]
    what is this called? ¿cómo se llama esto?
    call box una cabina telefónica [. . . teh-leh-
fonnee-ka]
calm tranquilo [trank*ee*loh]
    calm down tranquilícese [trankee-*lee*-
theh-seh]
camera una máquina de fotos [m*a*keena . . .]
camino cerrado road closed
camp: is there somewhere we can camp?
¿hay algún sitio donde podamos acamp*a*r?
[eye alg*oo*n s*ee*t-yoh . . .]
    can we camp here? ¿se puede acamp*a*r aquí?
[seh pw*eh*-deh . . . ak*ee*]
    we're on a camping holiday estamos de
camping
    campsite un camping
» *TRAVEL TIP: camping carnet not essential; if
camping off-site ask permission wherever
possible*
can¹: a can of beer una lata de cerveza [l*ah*-
tadeh therveh-tha]
    can-opener un abrelatas [ah-brehl*ah*-tas]
can²: can I have . . . ? ¿me da . . . ? [meh da]
    can you show me . . . ? ¿podría enseñarme . . . ?
[pod-r*ee*-a ensen-y*a*r-meh]
    I can't . . . no puedo [noh pw*eh*-doh]
    I can't swim no sé nad*a*r [. . . seh . . .]
    he can't . . . no puede [noh pw*eh*-deh]
    we can't . . . no podemos [noh pod-*eh*-moss]
Canada Canad*á*
Canadian canadiense [–y*e*n-seh]
cancel anul*a*r
    I want to cancel my booking quiero anular
mi reserva [kee-*eh*-roh anool*a*r mee reh-
s*ai*rva]

can we cancel dinner for tonight?
¿podríamos no cenar aquí esta noche? [podree-amoss no theh-nar akee . . .]
candle una vela [veh-la]
  by candlelight a la luz de una vela [. . . looth . . .]
capsize volcarse [vol-kar-seh]
car un coche [koh-cheh]
carafe una garrafa
caravan una caravana
carburettor el carburador [–boo–]
cards las cartas
  do you play cards? ¿juega usted a las cartas? [hweh-ga oosteh . . .]
care: goodbye, take care adiós, cuídese [kweedeh-seh]
  will you take care of this for me? ¿puede usted guardarme esto? [pweh-deh oosteh gwar-dar-meh esstoh]
careful: be careful tenga cuidado [. . . kwee-dah-doh]
car ferry un ferry
car park un aparcamiento [–mee-entoh]
carpet la alfombra
carrot una zanahoria [thanna-oree-a]
carry llevar
  could you carry this for me? ¿podría usted llevarme esto? [pod-ree-a oosteh yeh-var-meh esstoh]
  carry-cot un capazo [kapah-thoh]
carving una talla [ta-ya]
case (suitcase) la maleta [malleh-tah]
cash dinero [dee-neh-roh]
  I haven't any cash no tengo dinero en efectivo [. . . effektee-voh]
  I'll pay cash voy a pagar al contado
  cash desk la caja [kah-ha]
  will you cash a cheque for me? ¿podría hacerme efectivo un cheque? [pod-ree-a athair-meh effektee-voh oon cheh-keh]

....

casino el casino
cassette una cassette
castle el castillo [kass-*tee*-yoh]
cat un gato
catch: where do we catch the bus? ¿dónde se coge el autobús? [d*o*n-deh seh ko-*h*eh el owtoh-bo*o*ss]
   he's caught a bug ha cogido una infección [ah ko-*hee*doh *oo*na eem-fekth-yon]
cathedral la catedr*a*l
Catholic católico
cauliflower una coliflor
cave una cueva [kweh-va]
ceiling el techo
celery apio [*a*h-pee-oh]
cellophane celofán [theh-loh-f*a*n]
centigrade centígrado [then-*tee*-gra-doh]
» *TRAVEL TIP: to convert C to F:* $\frac{C}{5} \times 9 + 32 = F$

centigrade	−5	0	10	15	21	30	36.9
fahrenheit	23	32	50	59	70	86	98.4

centimetre un centímetro [then-*tee*–]
» *TRAVEL TIP: 1 cm = 0.39 inches*
central central [thentr*a*l]
   with central heating con calefacción central [. . . kalleh-fakth-yon . . .]
centre el centro [th–]
   how do we get to the centre? ¿cómo se llega al centro? [. . . seh y*e*h-ga . . .]
centro ciudad city centre
cerrado closed
certain cierto [thee-*ai*r-toh]
   are you certain? ¿está usted seguro? [est*a* oost*e*h seh-g*oo*-roh]
certificate un certificado [th–]
   birth certificate partida de nacimiento [. . . nathee-mee-*e*ntoh]
chain una cadena [ka-d*e*h-na]
chair una silla [*see*-ya]
   chairlift telesilla [teleh–]

chambermaid una camarera [–reh-ra]

champagne champán

change: could you change this into pesetas? ¿puede cambiarme esto en pesetas? [pweh-deh kam-bee-ar-meh . . .]

I haven't any change no tengo nada suelto [. . . swell-toh]

do we have to change trains? ¿tenemos que cambiar de tren? [teh-neh-moss keh . . .]

I'll just get changed me voy a cambiar

» *TRAVEL TIP: changing money; look for 'cambio' sign; most banks accept a cheque with banker's card; write cheques in English; take your passport*

channel: the Channel el Canal de la Mancha

charge: what will you charge? ¿cuánto me va a cobrar? [kwanto meh . . .]

who's in charge? ¿quién está a cargo de esto? [kee-en . . .]

chart *(sea)* carta de navegación [. . . deh na-veh-gath-yon]

cheap barato

have you got something cheaper? ¿tiene alguna otra cosa más barata? [tee-eh-neh . . .]

cheat: I've been cheated me han engañado [meh an engan-yah-doh]

check: will you check? ¿quiere asegurarse? [kee-eh-reh asseh-goorar-seh]

I'm sure, I've checked estoy seguro, lo he comprobado [loh eh . . .]

will you check the total? ¿quiere repasar la suma? [kee-eh-reh . . .]

we checked in nos inscribimos [eenskreebeemoss]

we checked out dejamos el hotel [deh-ha-moss . . .]

cheek la mejilla [meh-hee-ya]

cheeky descarado

cheerio hasta luego [asta lweh-goh]

(toast) salud [saloo]

....

cheers *(thank you)* gracias [grath-yass]
  (toast) salud [saloo]
cheese queso [keh-soh]
  cheesecake tarta de queso
  say cheese sonría [son-ree-a]
chef el jefe de cocina [heh-feh deh ko-thee-na]
chemist's una farmacia [far-math-ya]
» *TRAVEL TIP: list of duty chemists (farmacia de*
  guardia) found on the door or in local press
cheque un cheque [cheh-keh]
  will you take a cheque? ¿aceptan cheques?
  [athep-tan . . .]
  cheque book talonario de cheques [talon-
  ar-yo . . .]
  cheque card tarjeta de banco [tar-heh-ta . . .]
» *TRAVEL TIP: see* **change**
chest el pecho
» *TRAVEL TIP: chest measurements*

UK	34	36	38	40	42	44	46
Spain	87	91	97	102	107	112	117

chewing gum chicle [cheek-leh]
chickenpox varicela [varee-theh-la]
child un niño [neen-yoh]
  children los niños
  children's portions medias porciones para
  niños [mehd-yass porth-yoness . . .]
» *TRAVEL TIP: children are welcome almost*
  everywhere as family life is very strong in Spain
chin la barbilla [bar-bee-ya]
china porcelana [por-theh-lah-na]
chips patatas fritas [. . . freetass]
  (casino) fichas [feechass]
chocolate chocolate [–lah-teh)
  a box of chocolates una caja de bombones
  [kah-ha]
  hot chocolate chocolate a la taza [tah-tha]
choke *(car)* el aire [eye-reh]
chop *(noun)* una chuleta [choo–]
  pork/lamb chop una chuleta de cerdo/de
  cordero [. . . thair-doh . . .]

Christian name nombre de pila [nombreh deh peela]

Christmas Navidad

happy Christmas Feliz Navidad [feleeth . . .]

» *TRAVEL TIP: Spaniards celebrate Christmas Eve, New Year's Eve and the 6th of January, when presents are given*

church una iglesia [ee-gleh-see-a]

where is the Protestant/Catholic Church? ¿dónde está la iglesia protestante/católica?

cider sidra [seedra]

cigar un puro [poo-roh]

cigarette un cigarillo [theegaree-yo]

would you like a cigarette? ¿quiere un cigarillo? [kee-eh-reh . . .]

tipped/plain cigarettes . . . con filtro/sin filtro

» *TRAVEL TIP: if you prefer mild tobacco ask for 'tabaco rubio'* [. . . roob-yo]

cine-camera un tomavistas

cinema el cine [theeneh]

circle un círculo [theerkooloh]

(cinema: seat) butaca de principal [. . . deh preen-theepal]

city una ciudad [thee-oo-da]

claim *(insurance)* una reclamación [–ath-yon]

clarify aclarar

clean *(adjective)* limpio [leemp-yo]

can I have some clean sheets? ¿quiere ponerme sábanas limpias? [kee-eh-reh ponairmeh . . .]

my room hasn't been cleaned today hoy no han limpiado mi habitación [oy no an leemp-yah-doh mee abbee-tath-yon]

it's not clean no está limpio

cleansing cream crema limpiadora

clear: I'm not clear about it no lo comprendo bien [. . . bee-en]

clever listo [lee-stoh]

climate el clima [kleema]

....

clip *(ski)* un gancho
cloakroom el guardarropa [gwa–]
  (W.C.) los aseos [asseh-oss]
clock el reloj [reh-loh]
close cerca [thair-ka]
  (weather) bochorno
close: when do you close? ¿a qué hora se
  cierra? [ah keh ora seh thee-erra]
closed cerrado [th–]
cloth tela; *(rag)* un trapo
clothes la ropa
cloud una nube [noobeh]
clutch *(car)* el embrague [embra-gheh]
  the clutch is slipping patina el embrague
coach un autocar [ow–]
  coach party un grupo en autocar
coast la costa
  coastguard un guardacostas [gwa–]
coat un abrigo [–bree–]
coche-restaurante *dining car*
cockroach una cucaracha
coffee café
  white coffee/black coffee café con leche/café
  solo [. . . kon leh-cheh . . .]
coin una moneda [moneh-da]
cold frío [free-oh]
  I'm cold tengo frío
  I've got a cold tengo un resfriado
collapse: he's collapsed ha sufrido un colapso
  [ah soofreedoh]
collar el cuello [kweh-yo]
» *TRAVEL TIP: collar sizes*

(old) UK:	14	14½	15	15½	16	16½	17
Spanish:	36	37	38	39	41	42	43

collar bone la clavícula [–eekoo–]
collect: I want to collect . . . quería recoger . . .
  [keh-ree-a reh-kohair]
colour color
  have you any other colours? ¿lo tiene en
  otros colores? [. . . tee-eh-neh . . .]

comb un peine [pay-neh]
come venir [veneer]
  I come from London soy de Londres
  we came here yesterday llegamos ayer
  [yeh-gamoss ah-yair]
  come on! ¡vamos! [bah-moss]
  come with me venga conmigo [. . . kon-meegoh]
comedor *dining room*
comfortable cómodo
  it's not very comfortable no es muy cómodo
  [. . . mwee . . .]
Common Market el Mercado Común [mair-kah-doh kommoon]
communication cord el timbre de alarma
  [teembreh . . .]
company compañía [kompan-yee-ah]
  you're good company es usted una compañía
  agradable [. . . oosteh . . . agradah-bleh]
compartment *(train)* un compartimento
compass una brújula [broo-hoo-la]
compensation una indemnización [–thath-yon]
  I demand compensation exijo una
  indemnización [eggs-eehoh . . .]
complain quejarse [keh-harseh]
  **I want to complain about my room/the
  waiter** quiero presentar una queja sobre mi
  habitación/el camarero [kee-eh-ro . . . keh-ha
  soh-breh mee abbee-tath-yon]
  have you got a complaints book? ¿tiene
  usted un libro de reclamaciones? [tee-eh-neh
  oosteh oon leebroh deh reklamath-yoness]
completely completamente [–teh]
completo *no vacancies*
complicated: it's very complicated es muy
  complicado [. . . mwee . . .]
compliment: my compliments to the chef
  felicite al jefe de cocina de mi parte
  [feleetheeteh al heh-feh deh ko-theena deh mee
  parteh]

....

concert un concierto [kon-thee-*air*-toh]
concussion una conmoción cerebral [konmoth-yon thereh-bral]
condition la condición [kondeeth-yon]
 it's not in very good condition no está en muy buenas condiciones [. . . mw*ee* bweh-nass kon-deeth-yoness]
conference un congreso
confession una confesión [konfess-yon]
confirm confirmar [konfeerm*a*r]
confuse: you're confusing me me deja usted hecho un lío [meh d*e*h-*h*a oost*e*h *e*h-cho oon l*ee*-oh]
congratulations! ¡enhorabuena! [enora-bweh-na]
conjunctivitis conjuntivitis [kon-*h*oontee*vee*teess]
connection *(travel)* el enlace [en-l*a*h-theh]
connoisseur un experto [–p*air*–]
conscious consciente [kons-thee-*e*nteh]
consciousness: he's lost consciousness ha perdido el conocimiento [ah pairdeedoh el konotheem-yentoh]
conserje porter
consigna left luggage
constipation estreñimiento [esstren-yeem-yentoh]
consul el cónsul
consulate el consulado
contact: how can I contact . . .? ¿cómo puedo ponerme en contacto con . . .? [. . . pweh-doh pon-*ai*rmeh . . .]
 contact lenses lentes de contacto [lentess . . .
contraceptive un anticonceptivo [–thept*ee*voh
convenient conveniente [konven-yenteh]
cook: it's not cooked no está cocido [ko-thee-doh]
 it's beautifully cooked está guisado maravillosamente [. . . ghee-s*a*h-doh maravee-yosa-menteh]

you're a good cook es usted un buen cocinero [ess oosteh oon bwen kotheeneh-roh]

cooker una cocina [kotheena]

cool fresco

corkscrew un sacacorchos

corn *(foot)* un callo [ka-yoh]

corner: on the corner en la esquina [ess-keena]

in the corner en el rincón

can we have a corner table? ¿puede darnos una mesa cerca de un rincón? [pweh-deh . . . meh-sa thair-ka . . .]

cornflakes copos de maíz [. . . mah-eeth]

correct correcto

cosmetics cosméticos

cost: what does it cost? ¿cuánto cuesta? [kwantoh kwessta]

that's too much es demasiado caro [demass-yah-doh]

I'll take it me lo llevo [meh loh yeh-voh]

cotton algodón

cotton wool algodón

couchette litera [leeteh-ra]

cough *(noun)* tos [toss]

cough drops pastillas para la tos [pass-teeyass . . .]

cough medicine una medicina para la tos [meddee-theena . . .]

could: could you please . . . ? ¿podría usted . . . ? [podree-a oosteh . . .]

could I have . . . ? quiero . . . [kee-eh-roh]

country país [pa-eess]

in the country en el campo

couple: a couple of . . . un par de . . .

courier el guía turístico [ghee-a . . .]

course *(of meal)* un plato

of course por supuesto [. . . soopwestoh]

court: I'll take you to court voy a demandarle a usted [boy ah deh-mandar-leh ah oosteh]

cousin: my cousin mi primo [. . . pree—]

cover: **keep him covered** manténgale abrigado [–ga-leh . . .]
   cover charge el precio del cubierto [preth-yo del koob-yairtoh]
cow una vaca
crab un cangrejo [kangreh-hoh]
craft shop una tienda de artesanía [tee-enda deh artessanee-a]
crash: **there's been a crash** ha habido un accidente [ah abeedoh oon ak-theedenteh]
   crash helmet un casco
crazy loco
   you're crazy está usted loco [. . . oosteh . . .]
cream crema [kreh-ma]
crèche una guardería infantil [gwar-deh-ree-a . . .]
credit card una tarjeta de crédito [tar-heh-ta . . .]
crisis crisis [kree-seess]
crisps patatas fritas a la inglesa [freetass]
crossroads un cruce [kroo-theh]
crowded atestado
cruce crossroads
cruise un crucero [krootheh-roh]
crutch una muleta [moo–]
   (of body) las ingles [eengless]
cry llorar [yorrar]
   don't cry no llore [noh yo-reh]
cup una taza [tatha]
   a cup of coffee un café
cupboard un armario [armar-yoh]
curry 'curry' [koo–]
curtains las cortinas
cushion un cojín [ko-heen]
Customs la aduana [ad-wah-na]
cut: **I've cut myself** me he cortado [meh eh . . .]
cycle: **can we cycle there?** ¿se puede ir en bicicleta? [seh pweh-deh eer en beetheekleh-ta]
cyclist un ciclista [theekleesta]
cylinder el cilindro [theeleendroh]

cylinder-head gasket la junta de culata
[*h*oonta deh kool*a*h-ta]
dad(dy) papá
damage: I'll pay for the damage pagaré los
desperfectos [−re*h* . . .]
it's damaged es defectuoso [−too-*o*soh]
damas ladies
damn! ¡maldita sea! [mal-d*ee*-ta s*e*h-a]
damp húmedo [*oo*meh-doh]
dance: is there a dance on? ¿va a haber baile?
[ba ab*ai*r bye-leh]
would you like to dance? ¿bailas conmigo?
[bye-lass konm*ee*goh]
dangerous peligroso
dark oscuro [−k*oo*−]
dark blue azul oscuro [ath*oo*l . . .]
when does it get dark? ¿a qué hora oscurece?
[ah keh *o*ra oss-koor*e*h-theh]
darling querido [keh-r*ee*doh]
(to woman) querida
dashboard el cuadro [kw*a*−]
date: what's the date? ¿qué fecha es hoy?
[keh . . .]
it's the eighteenth of June es el dieciocho de
junio [. . . dee-ethee-*o*tcho deh *h*oon-yoh]
in 1982 en mil novecientos ochenta y dos [meel
noveh-thee-*e*ntoss otch*e*nt-eye-d*o*ss]
can we make a date? ¿podemos citarnos?
[pod*e*h-moss theet*a*r-noss]
dates *(fruit)* dátiles [d*a*h-teeless]
» *TRAVEL TIP: to say the date in Spanish you just use
the ordinary number (see pages 127–128), the
exception being:* **the first** el primero
daughter: my daughter mi hija [mee *ee*-h*a*]
day el día [d*ee*-a]
the day after el día de después [. . . dess-
pw*e*ss]
the day before el día de antes [. . . *a*ntess]
dazzle: his lights were dazzling me me
deslumbraban sus faros

dead muerto [moo-*ai*rtoh]
deaf sordo
  deaf-aid un aparato del oído [o-*ee*doh]
deal un negocio [neg*o*th-yoh]
  it's a deal trato hecho [. . . *e*tchoh]
  will you deal with it? ¿puede usted ocuparse
  de ello?
  [pweh-deh oost*e*h okkoop*a*r-seh deheh-yoh]
dear *(expensive)* caro
  Dear Sir muy señor mío
  Dear Madam estimada señora
  Dear Francisco querido Francisco
  (written by a man) mi querido amigo
December diciembre [deeth-y*e*mbreh]
deck la cubierta [koob-y*ai*rta]
  deckchair una tumbona [toom–]
declare: I have nothing to declare no tengo
  nada que declar*a*r [. . . keh . . .]
deep profundo
  is it deep? ¿es muy profundo? [. . . mwee . . .]
defendant el acusado [–koo–]
de-icer un deshelador [dess-eh-lad*o*r]
delay: the flight was delayed el vuelo se
  retras*ó* [vweh-loh seh reh–]
deliberately a propósito
delicate *(health)* delicado
delicatessen 'delicatessen'
delicious delicioso [deleeth-y*o*soh]
delivery el reparto [reh–]
  is there another mail delivery? ¿hay otro
  reparto de correo? [eye . . . korr*e*h-oh]
de luxe de lujo [deh l*o*o-*h*oh]
democratic democrático
demonstration *(of gadget etc)* una demostración
  [–ath-y*o*n]
dent una abolladura [aboya-d*o*ora]
  you've dented my car me ha abollado usted
  el coche [meh ah aboyy*a*h-doh oost*e*h el
  k*o*tcheh]
dentist un dentista

YOU MAY HEAR...
  abra todo lo que pueda – *open wide*
  enjuáguese [en-*h*wah-gheh-seh] – *rinse out*
dentures dentadura postiza [... poss-*tee*tha]
deny: I deny it lo niego [... nee-*e*h-goh]
deodorant un desodora*n*te [–teh]
departure la salida [–*ee*da]
depend: it depends (on ...) depende
  (de) ... [deh-p*e*ndeh deh]
deport deport*a*r [deh–]
deposit un depósito [deh–]
  do I have to leave a deposit? ¿hay que dejar
  un depósito? [eye keh deh*a*r ...]
depressed deprimido
depth profundidad
despacho de billetes *ticket office*
desperate: I'm desperate for a drink me
  muero por una copa [meh mw*e*h-roh ...]
dessert el postre [p*o*ss-treh]
destination dest*i*no
detergent un detergente [detair-*h*enteh]
desvío *diversion*
detour un rodeo [rod*e*h-oh]
devalued devaluado [–w*a*h-doh]
develop: could you develop these? ¿podría
  revelármelas? [podr*ee*-a reh-vel*a*r-meh-lass]
diabetic diab*é*tico
dialling code el prefijo [pref*ee*-*h*oh]
diamond un diamante [dee-ah-m*a*nteh]
diarrhoea diarrea [dee-arr*e*h-a]
  have you got something for diarrhoea?
  ¿tiene usted algo para la diarrea? [tee-*e*h-neh
  oost*e*h ...]
» *TRAVEL TIP: usually caused by cold drinks or*
  change of diet; drink tea or fresh lemon juice; eat
  only boiled rice, ham, apples, no fats
diary una agenda [ah-*h*enda]
dictionary un diccionario [deekth-yon*a*r-yoh]
die morir [mor*ee*r]; **he's dying** se est*á*
  muriendo [seh ... moor-y*e*ndoh]

....

didn't *see* **not**
diesel *(fuel)* gas-oil
diet dieta [dee-*e*h-ta]
  I'm on a diet est*o*y a dieta
different: they are different son diferentes
  can I have a different room? quisiera otra
  habitación distinta [keess-yeh-ra otra
  abbee-tath-yon . . .]
difficult difícil [dee*f*eetheel]
digestion la digestión [dee-*h*est-yon]
dinghy una barquita [–*k*ee–]
dining room el comedor [kommeh-d*o*r]
dinner la cena [theh-na]
  (lunch) el almuerzo [alm*w*air-thoh]
  dinner jacket un smoking
» *TRAVEL TIP: dinner normally available 9–11 pm*
dipped headlights luces cortas [*l*oothess . . .]
dirección única one-way *(street)*
direct *(adjective)* directo [dee–]
  does it go direct? ¿va directo?
dirty sucio [s*o*oth-yoh]
disabled minusválido [mee-nooss–]
disappear desaparecer [–eth*a*ir]
  it's just disappeared se ha debido esfumar
  [seh ah deb*ee*doh ess-foom*a*r]
disappointing decepcionante [deth-epth-
  yon*a*nteh]
disco una discot*e*ca; **see you in the disco** te
  veré en la discoteca [teh veh-reh . . .]
discount una rebaja [reb*a*h-*h*a]
disgusting asqu*e*roso [asskeh–]
dish un plato
dishonest poco honrado [. . . on–]
disinfectant un desinfect*a*nte [–teh]
dispensing chemist una farmacia [farm*a*th-ya]
distance la distancia [–thee-a]
  in the distance a lo lejos [. . . l*e*h-*h*oss]
distilled water agua destil*a*da [*a*hg-wa . . .]
distress signal una llamada de socorro
  [yam*a*h-da . . .]

distributor *(car)* el distribuidor [–weedor]
disturb: the noise is disturbing us nos está
molestando el ruido [. . . roo-eedoh]
divorced divorciado [deevorth-yado]
do: how do you do? hola, ¿qué tal? [oh-la
keh . . .]
what are you doing tonight? ¿qué vas a
hacer esta noche? [keh vass athair . . .]
how do you do it? ¿cómo se hace? [. . . seh
ah-theh]
will you do it for me? ¿me lo quiere hacer
usted? [. . . kee-eh-reh athair oosteh]
I've never done it before no lo he hecho en mi
vida [. . . eh eh-tchoh . . .]
he did it lo hizo [loh ee-thoh]
I was doing 60 kph iba a sesenta kilómetros
por hora [eeba ah . . . ora]
doctor el médico
I need a doctor necesito un médico
[nethesseetoh . . .]
» *TRAVEL TIP: look under 'Médicos' in the Yellow
Pages or find nearest 'Casa de Socorro'*
YOU MAY HEAR . . .
¿ha tenido esto antes? [ah teneedoh . . .] *have
you had this before?*
¿dónde le duele? [dondeh leh dweh-leh] *where
does it hurt?*
¿está tomando algún medicamento? *are you
taking any drugs?*
tómese una/dos de estas cada tres horas/al
día/dos veces al día *take one/two of these every
three hours/every day/twice a day*
document un documento [–koo–]
dog un perro
don't! ¡no lo haga! [. . . ah-ga] *see* **not**
door una puerta [pwair-ta]
dosage una dosis [doh-seess]
double: double room una habitación doble
[abbee-tath-yon doh-bleh]
double whisky un whisky doble

....

down: get down! ¡baje! [bah-heh]
   downstairs abajo [abah-hoh]
drain un sumidero [soo-mee-deh-roh]
drawing pin una chincheta
dress un vestido [−teedoh]
» *TRAVEL TIP: dress sizes*

UK	10	12	14	16	18	20
Spain	38	40	42	44	46	48

dressing *(for wound)* vendaje [vendah-heh]
   (for salad) aliño [aleen-yoh]
dressing gown una bata
drink *(verb)* beber [bebair]
   (alcoholic) una copa
   would you like something to drink? ¿quiere
   usted beber algo? [kee-eh-reh oosteh . . .]
   I don't drink no bebo [. . . beh-boh]
   is the water drinkable? ¿es potable el agua?
   [ess potah-bleh el ahg-wa]
drive: I've been driving all day llevo todo el
   día conduciendo [yeh-voh todoh el dee-a
   kondooth-yendoh]
driver el conductor [−dook−]
driving licence el permiso de conducir [pair-
   mee-soh deh kondoo-theer]
» *TRAVEL TIP: driving in Spain; you will need*
   international licence, registration documents
   and green card; seat belts compulsory out of
   town; red triangle and spare set of bulbs legal
   requirements
drown: he's drowning se está ahogando [seh
   essta ah-o-gandoh]
drug un medicamento
drunk borracho
dry seco [seh-koh]
   dry-clean limpieza en seco [leemp-yetha . . .]
ducha *shower*
due: when is the bus due? ¿a qué hora debe
   llegar el autobús? [ah keh ora deh-beh yeh-gar
   el ow-tobooss]
during durante [doo-ranteh]

dust polvo
duty-free el 'duty-free'
dynamo la dinamo [deen*ah*-moh]
each: can we have one each? ¿nos da uno a cada uno?
  how much are they each? ¿cuánto es cada uno? [kw–...]
ear la oreja [or*eh-h*a]
  I have earache tengo dolor de oídos [...deh o-*ee*doss]
early temprano
  we want to leave a day earlier queremos irnos un día antes de lo previsto [keh-*reh*-moss *eer*-noss oon d*ee*-a *a*ntess deh loh preh-v*ee*stoh]
earring un pendiente [–*yen*teh]
east este [*ess*teh]
easy fácil [f*ah*-theel]
Easter Semana Santa
eat comer [–*air*]
  something to eat algo de comer
egg un huevo [w*eh*-voh]
Eire Eire [*ay*-reh]
either: either ... or ... o ... o ...
  I don't like either no me gusta ninguno
elastic elástico
  elastic band una gomita [–*ee*ta]
elbow el codo
electric eléctrico
  electric blanket una manta eléctrica
  electric fire una estufa eléctrica [esst*oo*-fa...]
electrician un electricista [–*eethee*–]
electricity electricidad [elektreethee*da*]
elegant elegante [–teh]
else: something else algo más
  somewhere else en otra parte [...–teh]
  let's go somewhere else vamos a otra parte
  who else? ¿quién más? [kee-*en*...]
  or else si no [see...]
embarrassing violento [vee–]

embarrassed avergonzado [ah-vair-gon-th*a*h-doh]

embassy la embajada [emba*h*ada]

emergency una emergencia [em-air-*h*en-thee-ah]

empty vacío [–th*ee*–]

empuje *push*

encienda los faros *headlights on*

enclose: I enclose . . . adjunto . . . [–*h*oon–]

end el fin*a*l

  when does it end? ¿cuándo termina? [kw*a*ndoh tairm*ee*na]

engaged *(toilet)* ocupado [–k*oo*–]

  (telephone) comunicando [–m*oo*nee–]

  (person) prometido [–t*ee*–]

engagement ring el anillo de promet*i*da [an*ee*-yoh . . .]

engine el mot*o*r

  I've got engine trouble le pasa algo al mot*o*r [leh . . .]

England Inglaterra

English inglés [eengl*e*ss]

  the English los ingleses [eengl*e*h-sess]

enjoy: I enjoyed it very much me gustó mucho [meh goo-st*o*h m*oo*-choh]

enlargement *(photo)* una ampliación [ampl*ee*-ath-yon]

enormous enorme [eh-n*o*r-meh]

enough suficiente [s*oo*-feeth-y*e*nteh]

  thank you, that's enough gracias, es suficiente

entertainment diversiones [deevairs-y*o*h-ness]

entrada libre *admission free*

entrance la entr*a*da

entry la entr*a*da

envelope un sobr*e* [s*o*h-breh]

equipment equipo [eh-k*e*e-poh]

error un err*o*r

escalator una escalera mecánica [ess-kal*e*h-ra meh-k*a*nnika]

escuela *school*
especially especialmente [esspeth-yal-menteh]
espere *wait*
essential imprescindible [eempress-theen-
deebleh]
  it is essential that... es necesario que... [ess
nethessar-yoh keh]
estacionamiento limitado *restricted parking*
Europe Europa [eh-ooroh-pa]
evacuate desocupar [dessockoopar]
even: even the British hasta los británicos
[assta ...]
evening la tarde [tar-deh]
  (after nightfall) la noche [notch-eh]
  good evening buenas tardes [bweh-nass
tardess]
  this evening esta tarde/noche
  in the evening por la tarde
  evening dress traje de etiqueta [trah-heh deh
ettee-keh-ta]
  (woman's) traje de noche
ever: have you ever been to ...? ¿ha estado
alguna vez en ...? [ah esstah-doh al-goona veth
en]
every cada
  every day todos los días [... dee-ass]
  everyone todos
  everything todo
  everywhere en todas partes [... partess]
evidence pruebas [prweh-bass]
exact exacto [eggs-aktoh]
example un ejemplo [ehem–]
  for example por ejemplo
excellent excelente [ess-thellenteh]
except: except me menos yo [meh-noss ...]
excess exceso [ess-theh-soh]
  excess baggage exceso de equipaje [... deh
eckee-paheh]
exchange *(money)* cambio [kam-bee-oh]
  (telephone) Central Telefónica [th– ...]

exciting emocionante [emoth-yon*a*nteh]
excursion una excursión [ess-koors-yon]
excuse me *(to get past etc)* con permiso [...
  pair-m*ee*-soh]
  (to get attention) ¡por favor!
  (apology) perdone [pair-d*o*h-neh]
exhaust *(car)* el tubo de escape (*too*-boh deh
  ess-k*a*h-peh]
exhausted agot*a*do
exhibition una exposición [–seeth-yon]
exhibitor el expositor [ess-possee-t*o*r]
exit la salida [–l*ee*–]
expect: she's expecting est*á* esperando un
  niño [... n*ee*n-yoh]
expenses: it's on expenses esto corre a cargo
  de la compañía [... korreh ... kompan-y*ee*-a]
expensive caro
expert experto [ess-p*a*ir-toh]
explain explic*a*r
  would you explain that slowly? ¿podr*í*a
  explicar eso lentamente? [podr*ee*-a esspleek*a*r
  *e*h-so lenta-m*e*nteh]
export *(noun)* exportación [essport*a*th-yon]
exposure meter el fotómetro
express *(mail)* urgente [oor-*h*enteh]
extra: an extra glass otro vaso más [... v*a*h-
  soh ...]
  is that extra? ¿eso es extra?
extremely extremadamente [esstreh-mah-
  dam*e*nteh]
eye un ojo [*o*ho]
  eyebrow una ceja [th*e*h-*h*a]
  eye shadow sombra de ojos [*o*hoss]
  eye witness un testigo presencial [tesst*ee*goh
  pressenth-y*a*l]
face la cara
  face mask unas gafas de bucear [... deh
  booth*e*h-*a*r]
fact un hecho [*e*tcho]
factory una f*á*brica

Fahrenheit 'Fahrenheit'
» *TRAVEL TIP: to convert F to C:*

$$F -32 \times \frac{5}{9} = C$$

Fahrenheit	23	32	50	59	70	86	98.4
centigrade	−5	0	10	15	21	30	36.9

faint: she's fainted se ha desmayado [seh ah dess-ma-yah-doh]

fair *(fun-)* una verbena [vair-beh-na]
  (commercial) una feria [feh-ree-a]
  that's not fair no hay derecho [noh eye dereh-choh]

faithfully: yours faithfully le saluda atentamente

fake *(noun)* una falsificación [–ath-yon]

fall: he's fallen se ha caído [seh ah kah-ee-doh]

false falso [fal-soh]
  false teeth dientes postizos [dee-entess poss-tee-thoss]

family la familia [fameel-ya]

fan *(mechanical)* un ventilador
  (hand held) un abanico [–nee–]
  (football etc) un fan
  fan belt la correa del ventilador [korreh-ah . . .]

far lejos [leh-hoss]
  is it far? ¿está lejos?
  how far is it? ¿a qué distancia está [ah keh dee-stanth-ya . . .]

fare *(travel)* el billete [bee-yeh-teh]

farm una granja [gran-ha]

farther más allá [mass a-yah]

fashion la moda

fast rápido
  don't speak so fast no hable tan de prisa [noh ah-bleh tan deh pree-sa]

fat *(adjective)* gordo
  (on meat) grasa

fatal mortal

father: my father mi padre [mee pah-dreh]

....

fathom una braza [–th–]
fault *(defect)* un defecto
  it's not my fault no es culpa mía [k*oo*lpa m*ee*-a]
faulty defectuoso [deh-fekt-w*o*h-soh]
favourite favorito [fah-vor*ee*-toh]
February febrero [feh-breh-roh]
fed up: I'm fed up ¡estoy harto! [*ar*-toh]
feel sentir [–t*eer*]
  I feel hot/cold tengo calor/frío [fr*ee*-oh]
  I feel sad estoy triste [tr*ee*ss-teh]
  I feel like . . . tengo ganas de . . . [. . . deh]
ferry el ferry
fetch: will you come and fetch me? ¿quiere venir a buscarme? [kee-*e*h-reh ven*ee*r ah boosk*ar*-meh]
fever fiebre [fee-*e*h-breh]
few: only a few solo unos pocos
  a few days unos días [. . . d*ee*–]
fiancé: my fiancé mi novio [mee n*o*h-vee-oh]
fiancée: my fiancée mi novia
fiddle: it's a fiddle aquí hay trampa [ak*ee* eye . . .]
field un campo
fifty-fifty a medias [ah m*e*h-dee-ass]
figs higos [*ee*-goss]
figure una figura [–g*oo*–]
  (number) cifra [th*ee*–]
  I'm watching my figure estoy cuidando la línea [. . . kweed*a*ndoh la l*ee*neh-a]
fill: fill her up llénelo [yeh-neh-loh]
  to fill in a form rellenar un impreso [reh-yeh-n*a*r oon eempreh-soh]
fillet un filete [fee-l*e*h-teh]
film una película [peh-l*ee*-koola]
  do you have this type of film? ¿tiene películas de este tipo? [tee-*e*h-neh peh-l*ee*-koolass deh *e*ss-teh t*ee*-poh]
filter filtro [f*ee*l–]; **filter or non-filter?** ¿con o sin filtro? [. . . seen . . .]

final de autopista *end of motorway*

find encontrar

if you find it ... si lo encuentra ... [see loh enkwentra]

I've found a ... he encontrado un ... [eh ...]

fine *(weather)* bueno [bweh-noh]

a 3,000 peseta fine una multa de tres mil pesetas [... meel peh-seh-tass]

OK, that's fine vale, muy bien [bah-leh, mwee bee-en]

finger un dedo [deh-doh]

fingernail una uña [oon-ya]

finish: I haven't finished no he terminado [no eh tairmeenah-doh]

fire: fire! ¡fuego! [fweh-goh]

can we light a fire here? ¿se puede encender fuego aquí? [seh pweh-deh enthen-dair fweh-goh akee]

it's not firing *(car)* no da chispa [... chee–]

fire brigade los bomberos [bombeh-ross]

fire extinguisher un extintor [ess-teen-tor]

» TRAVEL TIP: *number for fire brigade will be in front of phone directory*

firme deslizante *slippery surface*

first el primero [pree-meh-roh]

I was first yo soy el primero

first aid primeros auxilios [pree-meh-ross ah-ook-seel-yoss]

first aid kit un botiquín [–keen]

first class primera clase [... –seh]

first name nombre de pila [nombreh deh peela]

fish un pez [peth]; *(food)* pescado

fishing la pesca

fishing rod una caña de pescar [kan-ya deh ...]

fishing tackle un aparejo de pesca [apareh-hoh deh ...]

fix: can you fix it? *(arrange, repair)* ¿lo puede arreglar? [pweh-deh ...]

fizzy con gas
flag una bandera [–d*e*h–]
flash *(phot)* flash
flat llano [y*a*h-noh]
   this drink is flat esta bebida está floja [. . .
   flo-h*a*]
   I've got a flat (tyre) tengo una (rueda)
   deshinchada [. . . rw*e*h-da dess-eench*a*h-da]
   I'm looking for a flat estoy buscando un piso
   [. . . p*ee*-soh]
flavour sabor
flea una pulga [p*oo*–]
flies *(on trousers)* la bragueta [–gh*e*h–]
flight vuelo [vw*e*h-loh]
flippers aletas
flirt *(verb)* coquetear [kockeh-teh-*a*r]
float *(verb)* flot*a*r
floor el suelo [sw*e*h-loh]
   on the second floor en el segundo piso [. . .
   p*ee*-soh]
flower una flor
flu gripe [gr*ee*-peh]
fly *(insect)* una mosca
foggy: it's foggy hay niebla [eye nee-*e*h-bla]
follow seguir [–gh*ee*r]
food comida [komm*ee*da]
   food poisoning intoxicación alimenticia
   [intoxicath-y*o*n aleement*ee*th-ya]
fool tonto
foot un pie [pee-*e*h]
   football fú*t*bol
   (ball) un balón
» *TRAVEL TIP: 1 foot = 30.1 cm = 0.3 metres*
for para
forbidden prohibido [pro-eeb*ee*e-doh]
foreign extranjero [–h*e*h-roh]
   foreign exchange divisas [dee-v*ee*-sass]
foreigner un extranjero [–h*e*h-roh]
forest un bosque [b*o*ss-keh]
forget olvidar [olve-d*a*r]

I forget, I've forgotten no me acuerdo, me he olvidado [noh meh ak-wair-doh, meh eh . . .]
don't forget no se olvide [. . . –vee-deh]
I'll never forget you nunca te olvidaré [. . . teh olvee-dareh]
fork un tenedor
form *(document)* hoja [oh-ha]
formal formal
  (person) estirado [–tee–]
  (dress) de etiqueta [–eekeh–]
fortnight quince días [keen-theh dee-ass]
forward hacia adelante [ath-ya . . . –teh]
  could you forward my mail? ¿puede enviarme el correo a mi nueva dirección? [pweh-deh embee-armeh el korreh-oh ah mee nweh-va deerek-thee-on]
  forwarding address nueva dirección
foundation cream crema base [kreh-ma bah-seh]
fracture una fractura
fragile frágil [frah-heel]
France Francia [franth-ya]
fraud un fraude [fra-oo-deh]
free libre [lee-breh]
  admission free entrada gratis
freight mercancías [–thee-ass]
French francés [–thess]
freshen up: I want to freshen up quiero refrescarme [kee-eh-roh reh-freskar-meh]
Friday viernes [vee-air-ness]
fridge el frigorífico
fried egg un huevo frito [weh-voh free-toh]
friend un amigo [amee-goh]
friendly simpático
from de [deh]
  where is it from? ¿de dónde es?
front *(noun)* la parte delantera [parteh delanteh-ra]; **in front of you** delante de usted [delan-teh deh oosteh]; **at the front** por delante

....

frost escarcha
  frostbite congelación [kon-*h*eh-lath-yon]
frozen congelado [kon-*h*eh–]
fruit fruta [froo–]
fruit salad macedonia de frutas [mathed*o*n-ya deh . . .]
fry freír [freh-*ee*r]
  nothing fried nada frito [free–]
  frying pan una sartén
full lleno [yeh–]
fun: it's fun es divertido [deev-air-t*ee*doh]
funny *(strange)* raro
  (comical) gracioso [grath-yoh-soh]
furniture muebles [mweh-bless]
further más allá [. . . a-yah]
fuse el fusible [foo-*see*-bleh]
future futuro [f*oo*too-roh]
  in future en lo sucesivo [soo-thess-*ee*voh]
gale un vendaval
gallon un galón
» *TRAVEL TIP: 1 gallon = 4.55 litres*
gallstone un cálculo biliario [k*a*lkooloh beel-y*a*ree-oh]
gamble jugar [*h*oo–]
gammon jamón [h*a*–]
garage *(repair)* un taller [ta-y*a*ir]
  (petrol) una gasolinera [–*ee*neh-ra]
  (parking) un garage [gar*a*-*h*eh]
» *TRAVEL TIP: petrol stations rarely have a*
  mechanic – if in trouble try nearest 'taller'
garden el jardín [h*a*rdeen]
garlic ajo [*a*h-*h*o]
gas gas *(petrol)* gasolina [–lee–]
  gas cylinder una bombona de gas
gasket una junta [h*oo*–]
gay *(homosexual)* 'gay' [guy]
gear *(car)* marcha
  (equipment) equipo [–*kee*–]
  I have gearbox trouble le pasa algo a la caja de cambios [leh . . . k*a*h-*h*a deh k*a*mb-yoss]

....

gear lever la palanca de velocidades [. . . velothee-d*a*h-dess]
I can't get it into gear no le entra la marcha
gents los aseos [ass*e*h-oss]
gesture un gesto [*he*–]
get: will you get me a . . .? ¿me quiere busc*a*r un . . .? [kee-*e*h-reh . . .]
  how do I get to . . .? ¿cómo se va a . . .?
  when can I get it back? ¿cuándo puedo recogerlo? [. . . pw*e*h-doh reh-koh-*h*air-loh]
  where do I get off? ¿dónde tengo que bajarme? [. . . ba*h*armeh]
  when do we get back? ¿a qué hora volvemos? [ah keh *o*ra . . .]
  where can I get a bus for . . .? ¿dónde se coge el autobús para . . .? [d*o*ndeh seh k*o*h-*h*eh el ow-toh-b*oo*ss . . .]
  have you got . . .? ¿tiene usted . . .? [tee-*e*h-neh oost*e*h]
gin ginebra [*h*een*e*h-bra]
  gin and tonic una tónica con ginebra
girl una chica [ch*e*e-ka]
  my girlfriend mi amiga [mee . . .]
give dar
  will you give me . . .? ¿me quiere dar . . .? [meh kee-*e*h-reh . . .]
  I gave it to him se lo dí a él [. . . dee . . .]
glad al*e*gre [–greh]
  I'm glad me alegro
gland una gl*á*ndula [–doo–]
  glandular fever fiebre glandul*a*r [fee-*e*h-breh . . .]
glass cristal; *(drinking)* un vaso
  a glass of water un vaso de agua [*a*hg-wa]
glasses las gafas
gloves guantes [gw*a*ntess]
glue cola
go ir [eer]
  when does the bus go? ¿a qué hora sale el autobús [ah keh *o*ra s*a*h-leh el owtoh-b*oo*ss]

....

where are you going? ¿dónde va usted?
[d*o*ndeh va oost*e*h]
let's go vámonos [b*a*h-moh-noss]
go on! ¡vamos! [b–]
the bus has gone se nos ha ido el autobús
[. . . ah *ee*-doh . . .]
he's gone se ha ido [seh . . .]
can I have a go? ¿puedo prob*a*r yo?
[pw*e*h-doh . . .]
my car won't go mi coche no anda
goal un gol
goat una cabra
  goat's cheese queso de cabra [k*e*h-soh . . .]
God Dios [dee-*o*ss]
goggles *(ski)* gafas de esquí [. . . essk*ee*]
gold oro
golf el golf
good bueno [bw*e*h-noh]
  good! ¡muy bien! [mw*ee* bee-*e*n]
goodbye adiós
gooseberries grosellas [groh-s*e*h-yass]
gramme un gramo
» *TRAVEL TIP: 100 grammes = approx 3½ oz*
grand magnífico
  granddaughter nieta [nee-*e*hta]
  grandfather abuelo [abw*e*h-loh]
  grandmother abuela
  grandson nieto [nee-*e*htoh]
grapes uvas [*oo*vass]
grapefruit pomelo [–m*e*h–]
  grapefruit juice zumo de pomelo
  [th*oo*moh . . .]
grass hierba [y*ai*r-ba]
grateful agradecido [–deth*ee*-doh]
  I'm very grateful to you se lo agrad*e*zco
  mucho [. . . agrad*e*th-koh]
gratitude agradecimiento [–etheem-y*e*ntoh]
gravy salsa
grease grasa
greasy grasiento [grass-y*e*ntoh]

....

great grande [–deh]
  great! ¡estupendo! [estoopendoh]
greedy codicioso [–eethee–]
  (for food) glotón
green verde [vair-deh]
  greengrocer's la verdulería [vairdooleh-ree-a]
  green card carta verde
grey gris [greess]
grocer's la tienda de comestibles [tee-enda deh komess-tee-bless]
ground el suelo [sweh-loh]
  on the ground en el suelo
  on the ground floor en la planta baja [. . . bah-ha]
group un grupo [groo–]
  our group leader el guía de nuestro grupo [ghee-a deh nwesstroh . . .]
  I'm with the English group estoy en el grupo de los ingleses [. . . eengleh-sess]
guarantee la garantía [–tee-a]
  is there a guarantee? ¿tiene garantía? [tee-eh-neh . . .]
guest invitado [eembeetah-doh]
guesthouse casa de huéspedes [kah-sa deh wesspedess]
guide un guía [ghee-a]
guilty culpable [koolpah-bleh]
guitar una guitarra [gheetarra]
gum la encía [enthee-a]
gun una pistola
gynaecologist un ginecólogo [heeneh-kollogoh]
hair el pelo [peh-loh]
  hairbrush un cepillo para el pelo [theh-peel-yoh . . .]
  hair grip una horquilla [or-kee-ya]
  where can I get a haircut? ¿dónde puedo cortarme el pelo? [don-deh pweh-doh kortar-meh . . .]
  is there a hairdresser's here? ¿hay alguna

peluquería aquí? [eye algoona pelookeh-ree-ah akee]

half la mitad [la meetah]
  a half portion media porción [maid-ya porth-yon]
  half an hour media hora [maid-ya ora]
ham jamón de York [hamon . . .]
  hamburger una hamburguesa [amboorgheh-sa]
hammer un martillo [marteeyoh]
hand una mano
  handbag un bolso
  handbrake el freno de mano
handkerchief un pañuelo [pan-yweh-loh]
handle *(door)* el picaporte [–teh]
  (cup) el asa
hand luggage equipaje de mano [eckee-pahheh . . .]
hand-made hecho a mano [etcho . . .]
handsome guapo [gwah-poh]
hanger una percha [pair-cha]
hangover resaca
  my head is killing me parece que me va a estallar la cabeza [pareh-theh keh meh vah essta-yar la kabeh-tha]
happen suceder [sootheh-dair]
  I don't know how it happened no sé cómo sucedió [. . . seh . . . soothehd-yoh]
  what's happening/what's happened? ¿qué pasa/qué ha pasado? [keh ah . . .]
happy contento
harbour el puerto [pwair-toh]
hard duro [doo–]
  (difficult) difícil [deefeetheel]
  hard-boiled egg un huevo duro [weh-voh . . .]
  push hard empuje fuerte [empoo-heh fwairteh]
harm *(noun)* daño [dahn-yoh]
hat sombrero
hate: I hate . . . detesto . . .

....

have tener [ten*air*]
   I have no time no tengo tiempo [. . . tee-
   *e*mpoh]
   do you have any cigars/a map? ¿tiene usted
   puros/un mapa? [tee-*e*h-neh oost*e*h . . .]
   can I have some water/some more? ¿puede
   ponerme un poco de agua/un poco más?
   [pweh-deh poh-n*air*-meh . . .]
   I have to leave tomorrow tengo que irme
   mañana [. . . keh *eer*-meh man-y*a*h-na]
hay fever fiebre del heno [fee-*e*h-breh del *e*h-
noh]
he él
   does he live here? ¿vive aquí? [*vee*-veh ak*ee*]
   he is my friend es amigo mío [. . . m*ee*-oh]
   he is ill está enfermo [–f*air*–]
head la cabeza [–tha]
   headache dolor de cabeza
   headlight un faro
   head waiter el jefe de camareros [*h*eh-feh deh
   kamar*e*h-ross]
   head wind viento contrario [vee-*e*ntoh
   kontr*a*h-ree-oh]
health salud [sal*oo*]
   your health! ¡a tu salud! [ah too . . .]
healthy sano [s*a*h-noh]
hear: I can't hear no oigo [*oy*-goh]
   hearing aid un aparato del oído [o-*ee*doh]
heart el corazón [–th*o*n]
   heart attack un infarto
heat calor
   heat stroke una insolación [–l*a*th-yon]
heating calefacción [kaleh-f*a*kth-yon]
heavy pesado [peh-s*a*h-doh]
heel un tacón
   could you put new heels on these? ¿puede
   ponerles tapas nuevas? [pweh-deh pon*air*-less
   t*a*pass nweh-vass]
height altura [–*too*–]
hello! ¡hola! [*o*-la]

help ayuda [–*yoo*–]
  can you help me? ¿puede ayudarme? [pweh-deh ah-yoo-d*a*r-meh]
help! ¡socorro!
her: I know her la conozco [. . . kon*o*th-koh]
  will you give it to her? ¿quiere dárselo a ella? [kee-*e*h-reh d*a*rseh-loh a *e*h-ya]
  it's her es ella [ess *e*h-ya]
  it's her bag, it's hers es su bolso, es suyo [. . . *soo*-yoh]
here aquí [ak*ee*]
  come here venga aquí [b*e*nga . . .]
high alto
hill un monte [–teh]
  up/down the hill cuesta arriba/abajo [kw*e*sta arr*ee*ba/ab*a*h-*h*oh]
him: I know him le conozco [leh kon*o*th-ko]
  will you give it to him? ¿quiere dárselo a él? [kee-eh-reh . . .]
  it's him es él
hire *see* **rent**
his: it's his drink, it's his es su bebida, es suya [. . . s*oo*ya]
hit: he hit me me golpeó [golpeh-*o*h]
hitch-hike hacer autostop [ath*a*ir owtoh-stop]
  hitch-hiker un autostopista [owto-stop*ee*sta]
hold *(verb)* tener [ten*ai*r]
hole un agujero [agoo-*h*eh-roh]
holiday vacaciones [vacath-y*o*ness]
  I'm on holiday estoy de vacaciones
home casa [k*a*h-sa]
  I want to go home quiero irme a casa [kee-eh-roh *ee*r-meh . . .]
  at home en casa
  I'm homesick tengo morriña [morr*ee*n-ya]
honest honrado [on–]
  honestly? ¿de verdad? [deh vaird*a*]
honey miel [mee-*e*l]
honeymoon viaje de novios [vee-*a*h-*h*eh deh n*o*vee-oss]

hope *(noun)* esperanza [–*a*ntha]
  I hope that ... espero que ... [essp*e*h-roh keh]
  I hope so/not espero que sí/no
horas de visita *visiting hours*
horizon el horizonte [oreeth*o*nteh]
horn *(car)* el claxon
horrible horrible [orr*ee*bleh]
hors d'oeuvre entremeses [entreh-m*e*h-sess]
horse un caballo [–*a*-yoh]
hospital el hospital [ossp*ee*t*a*l]
  » *TRAVEL TIP: there are also First Aid Centres*
    called 'Casas de Socorro'
host el anfitrión [amfeetree-*o*n]
hostess la anfitriona
  (air) la azafata [atha–]
hot caliente [kal-y*e*nteh]
  (spiced) picante
hotel un hotel [oh-t*e*l]
hotplate *(on cooker)* la placa
hot-water bottle una bolsa de agua caliente [. . .
  *a*hg-wa kal-y*e*nteh]
hour una hora [*o*ra]
house una casa [k*a*h-sa]
  housewife ama de casa
how cómo
  how many cuántos [kw–]
  how much cuánto
  how often? ¿cada cuánto tiempo? [. . . tee-
  *e*mpoh]
  how long does it take? ¿cuánto se tarda?
  how long have you been here? ¿desde
  cuándo está usted aquí? [d*e*z-deh kw*a*ndoh esta
  oost*e*h ak*ee*]
  how are you? ¿como está usted? [. . . oost*e*h]
hull el casco
humid húmedo [*oo*meh-doh]
humour humor [*oo*m*o*r]
  you need a sense of humour hay que tener
  sentido del humor [eye keh ten*air* sent*ee*doh del
  *oo*m*o*r]

hundredweight un quintal *(approx)* [keent*a*l]
» *TRAVEL TIP: 1 cwt = 50.8 kilos*

hungry: I'm hungry/not hungry tengo/no
tengo hambre [. . . *a*mbreh]

hurry: I'm in a hurry tengo prisa [pr*ee*-sa]
please hurry! ¡de prisa, por favor!

hurt: it hurts me duele [meh dw*eh*-leh]
my leg hurts me duele la pierna [pee-*ai*r-na]
YOU MAY THEN HEAR . . .
¿es un dolor agudo? [. . . ag*oo*doh] *is it a sharp
pain?*

husband: my husband mi marido [mee
mar*ee*doh]

I yo
I am a doctor/British soy médico/británico
I am tired estoy cansado
I live in London vivo en Londres [v*ee*-vo . . .]

ice hielo [y*eh*-loh]
ice-cream un helado [eh-l*a*h-doh]
iced coffee café helado
with lots of ice con mucho hielo

identity papers los documentos de identidad
[dok*oo*mentoss deh eedentee-d*a*]

idiot idiota [eed-y*o*ta]

if si [see]

ignition el encendido [enth-end*ee*-doh]

ill enfermo [−f*ai*r−]
I feel ill me encuentro mal [. . .
enkwentroh . . .]

illegal ilegal [ee-leh-g*a*l]

illegible ilegible [ee-leh-*hee*bleh]

illness una enfermedad [enfairmeh-d*a*]

immediately ahora mismo [ah-ora m*ee*zmoh]

import *(verb)* importar

important importante [−teh]
it's very important es muy importante [. . .
m*wee* . . .]

import duty derechos de entrada

impossible imposible [−s*ee*bleh]

....

impressive impresionante [eempress-yon*a*nteh]
improve mejorar [me*h*orar]
   I want to improve my Spanish quiero
   perfeccionar mi español [kee-*e*h-roh
   pairfekth-yon*a*r mee ess-pan-y*o*l]
in en
inch una pulgada
» *TRAVEL TIP: 1 inch = 2.54 cm*
include incluír [een-klw*ee*r]
   does that include breakfast? ¿está
   comprendido el desayuno? [est*a* comprend*ee*doh
   el dess-ayoo-noh]
inclusive inclusive [eencloos*ee*veh]
incompetent incompetente [–teh]
inconsiderate desconsider*a*do
incontinent incontin*e*nte [–teh]
incredible increíble [een-kreh-*ee*bleh]
indecent indecente [een-deh-th*e*nteh]
independent independiente [–y*e*nteh]
India India
Indian hindú [een-d*oo*]
indicator el indicad*o*r
indigestion una indigestión [eendee-*h*est-yon]
indoors en casa [k*a*h-sah]
industry la industria [eend*oo*stree-a]
infection una infección [eenfekth-yon]
infectious infeccioso [eenfekth-yoh-soh]
inflation inflación [eenflath-yon]
Información *Information Office/Desk*
informal inform*a*l
   (person) natur*a*l [–too–]
information información [–ath-yon–]
   do you have any information in English
   about...? ¿tiene alguna información en inglés
   sobre ...? [tee-*e*h-neh algoona ... s*o*h-breh]
   is there an information office? ¿hay una
   oficina de información? [eye oona offee-th*ee*na
   deh ...]
inhabitant un habitante [abeet*a*nteh]
injection una inyección [een-yekth-yon]

injured herido [eh-ree-doh]
 he's been injured está herido
injury una herida [eh-ree-da]
innocent inocente [–thenteh]
insect un insecto
 insect repellent una loción
 ahuyentamosquitos [loth-yon ow-yenta–]
inside dentro de [. . . deh]
insist: I insist (on it) insisto (en ello) [. . . eh-
 yoh]
insomnia insomnio [een-somnee-oh]
instant coffee café instantáneo [eenstantah-
 neh-oh]
instead en cambio [kam-bee-oh]
 instead of . . . en lugar de . . . [en loogar deh]
insulating tape cinta aislante [theenta ah-
 eess-lanteh]
insulation aislamiento [ah-eeslam-yentoh]
insult un insulto [eensooltoh]
insurance el seguro [–goo–]
intelligent inteligente [eentellee-henteh]
interesting interesante [eenteh-reh-santeh]
international internacional [–nath-yonal]
interpret interpretar
 would you interpret for us? ¿podría usted
 hacer de intérprete nuestro? [podree-a oosteh
 ath-air deh eentair-preteh nwestroh]
into en
introduce: can I introduce . . .? permítame
 presentarle a . . . [pairmeeta-meh press-entar-
 leh ah]
invalid *(noun)* un inválido [eembalido]
 invalid chair una silla de inválido [see-yah
 deh . . .]
invitation una invitación [eembeetath-yon]
 thank you for the invitation gracias por la
 invitación
invite invitar [eembeetar]
 can I invite you out? ¿te gustaría salir
 conmigo? [teh goostaree-a saleer konmeegoh]

invoice la factura [–*too*–]
Ireland Irlanda [eer–]
Irish irlandés [eerland*ess*]
iron *(noun: clothes)* una plancha
  will you iron these for me? ¿puede
  planchármelos? [pweh-deh planch*a*r-meh-loss]
ironmonger's una ferretería [ferreh-terr*ee*-a]
is es, est*á*
island una isla [*eess*-la]
it lo
  it's not working no funciona [. . . foonth-
  y*oh*-na]
  give me it démelo [d*e*h-meh-loh]
  is it . . .? es . . .?, est*á* . . .?
itch pic*o*r
  it itches me pica [meh p*ee*-ka]
itemize: would you itemize it for me? ¿me lo
  puede desglosar? [meh loh pweh-deh
  dez-gloh-s*a*r]
jack el gato
jacket una chaqueta [chack*e*h-ta]
jam mermelada [mair-meh-l*a*h-da]
  traffic jam un atasco
January enero [en-*e*h-roh]
jaw la mandíbula [–d*ee*boo–]
jealous *(in love)* celoso [th–]
jeans unos vaqueros [vak*e*h-ross]
jellyfish una medusa [–d*oo*–]
jetty el muelle [mw*e*h-yeh]
jewellery joyas [*hoy*-yass]
jib el foque [f*o*h-keh]
job un trabajo [–*h*oh]
  just the job! ¡estupendo! [–*too*–]
joke *(noun)* un chiste [ch*ee*ss-teh]
  you must be joking ¿pero lo dice en serio?
  [peh-roh lo d*ee*theh en s*e*h-ree-oh]
journey un viaje [bee-*ah*eh]
  have a good journey ¡buen viaje! [bwem-
  bee-*ah*eh]
July julio [*hoo*l-yoh]

....

jumper un jersey [*h*air-s*a*y]
junction un cruce [kr*oo*-theh]
June junio [*h*oon-yoh]
junk baratijas [barat*ee*-h*a*ss]
just: just dos sólo dos
  just a little sólo un poquito [. . .pok*ee*toh]
  just there allí mismo [a-y*ee* m*ee*z-moh]
  not just now no en este momento
  just now ahora mismo [ah-*o*ra m*ee*zmoh]
  he was here just now estaba aquí hace un
  momento [. . .ak*ee* *a*h-theh . . .]
  that's just right as*í* está bién [bee-*e*n]
keen: I'm not keen no tengo ganas
keep: can I keep it? ¿puedo quedarme con él?
  [pweh-doh keh-d*a*r-meh . . .]
  you keep it quédese con él [k*e*h-deh-seh . . .]
  keep the change quédese con el cambio
  [k*e*h-deh-seh . . .]
  you didn't keep your promise usted no
  cumplió su promesa [oost*e*h noh koomplee-*o*h
  soo prom-*e*h-sa]
  it keeps on breaking se rompe una y otra vez
  [seh rompeh *oo*na ee *o*-tra veth]
key la llave [y*a*h-veh]
kidneys los riñones [reen-yoh-ness]
kill mat*a*r
kilo un kilo [k*ee*loh]

» *TRAVEL TIP: conversion:* $\dfrac{kilos}{5} \times 11 = pounds$

kilos	1	1½	5	6	7	8	9
pounds	2.2	3.3	11	13.2	15.4	17.6	19.8

kilometre un kilómetro [keelommetroh]

» *TRAVEL TIP: conversion:* $\dfrac{kilometres}{8} \times 5 = miles$

kilometres:	1	5	10	20	50	100
miles:	0.62	3.11	6.2	12.4	31	62

kind: that's very kind of you es usted muy
  amable [ess oost*e*h mwe am*a*h-bleh]
kiss un beso [beh-soh]
» *TRAVEL TIP: normal form of greeting between*

....

*female friends and often female and male
friends*

kitchen cocina [koth*ee*na]

knee una rodilla [rod*ee*-ya]

knickers unas bragas

knife un cuchillo [kooch*ee*-yoh]

knock un golpe [–peh]

  there's a knocking noise from the engine
suena un golpeteo en el motor [sweh-na oon
golpeh-t*eh*-oh . . .]

know saber [sab*air*]

  I don't know no sé [noh seh]

  I don't know the area no conozco la región
[noh kon*o*thko la reh-yon]

label una etiqueta [–eek*eh*-ta]

laces *(shoes)* cordones [kor-d*o*h-ness]

lacquer laca

ladies los aseos de señoras [ass-*eh*-oss deh
sen-yorass]

  lady una señora [sehn-yorah]

lager cerveza [thair-v*eh*-tha]

  lager and lime cerveza con lima [. . . l*ee*ma]

lamb *(meat)* cordero [–d*eh*–]

lamp una lámpara

  lampshade una pantalla [pant*a*-ya]

  lamp-post una farola

land *(noun)* tierra [tee-*e*rra]

lane *(car)* el carril [–*ee*l]

language idioma [eed-yoh-ma]

large grande [–deh]

laryngitis laringitis [lareen-h*ee*teess]

last último [*oo*l–]

  last year/week el año pasado/la semana
pasada [*a*n-yoh . . .]

  last night anoche [an*o*tcheh]

  at last! ¡al fin! [. . . feen]

late: sorry I'm late perdone que haya llegado
tarde [pairdoh-neh keh *a*h-ya yeh-g*a*h-doh
t*a*r-deh]

  it's a bit late es un poco tarde

please hurry, I'm late dése prisa, por favor, que llego tarde [deh-seh pree-sa . . . keh yeh-goh tardeh]

at the latest a más tardar

later más tarde

I'll come back later volveré más tarde [volveh-reh . . .]

see you later hasta luego [asta lweh-goh]

latitude latitud [–too]

laugh (verb) reír [reh-eer]

launderette una lavandería automática [–ree-a ow-toh-matteeka]

lavabos toilets

lavatory el wáter [vatair]

law la ley [lay]

lawyer un abogado

laxative un laxante [–teh]

lazy perezoso [peh-rethosoh]

leaf una hoja [oh-ha]

leak un agujero [agoo-heh-roh]

there's a leak in my ceiling tengo una gotera en el techo [. . . goh-teh-ra . . .]

the petrol tank leaks se sale la gasolina [seh sah-leh la gassoh-leena]

learn: I want to learn . . . quiero saber . . . [kee-eh-roh sab-air]

lease (verb) arrendar

least: not in the least de ninguna manera [deh neengoona maneh-ra]

at least por lo menos

leather cuero [kweh-roh]

this meat's like leather esta carne está como suela de zapato [. . . karneh . . . sweh-la deh thapah-toh]

leave: we're leaving tomorrow nos vamos mañana

when does the bus leave? ¿a qué hora sale el autobús? [ah keh ora sah-leh el ow-toh-booss]

I left two shirts in my room me dejé dos camisas en mi habitación [meh deheh doss

kam*ee*-sass en mee abbee-tath-yon]
can I leave this here? ¿puedo dejar esto aquí?
[pw*eh*-doh de*h*ar *e*stoh ak*ee*]
left izquierdo [eeth-kee-*air*-doh]
  on the left a la izquierda
  left-handed zurdo [th*oo*r-doh]
left luggage (office) la consigna de equipajes
[kons*ee*gna deh ekeep*ah-h*ess]
leg una pierna [pee-*air*-na]
legal legal [leh-g*a*l]
lemon un limón [lee–]
lemonade limonada [lee–]
lend: will you lend me your . . .? ¿quiere
prestarme su . . .? [kee-*eh*-reh presst*a*r-meh
soo]
lengthen alarg*a*r
lens *(phot)* el objetivo [ob-*h*eh-t*ee*voh]
Lent Cuaresma [kwarezma]
less menos [m*eh*-noss]
  less than three menos de tres [. . . deh . . .]
  less than that menos que eso [. . . keh . . .]
let: let me help déjeme ayudarle [d*eh*eh-meh
ah-yood*a*r-leh]
  let me go! ¡suélteme! [sw*ell*-teh-meh]
  will you let me off here? déjeme aquí, por
favor [d*eh*eh-meh ak*ee*]
  let's go vámonos [b*a*h-mo-noss]
letter una carta
  are there any letters for me? ¿hay cartas
para mí? [eye . . . mee]
  letterbox un buzón [boo-th*on*]
lettuce lechuga [–ch*oo*–]
level crossing un paso a nivel [. . . ah neev*e*l]
liable *(responsible)* responsable [–s*a*h-bleh]
library una biblioteca [beeb-lee-oh-t*eh*-ka]
licence el permiso [pair-m*ee*-soh]
lid la·tapa
lie *(noun)* una mentira [–t*ee*–]
  can he lie down for a bit? ¿puede acostarse
un rato? [pw*eh*-deh akosst*a*r-seh . . .]

....

life la vida [*vee*-da]
  life assurance un seguro de vida [seh-*goo*roh . . .]
  not at my time of life! ¡ya estoy viejo para eso! [. . . vee-*eh*-ho . . .]
  lifebelt, life-jacket un salvavidas [–*vee*dass]
  lifeboat una lancha salvavidas
  lifeguard un vigilante [vee*h*eelanteh]
lift: do you want a lift? ¿quiere que le lleve en mi coche? [kee-*eh*-reh keh leh *y*eh-veh en mee *k*otcheh]
  could you give me a lift? ¿podría llevarme en su coche? [pod-*ree*-ah yeh-*va*rmeh . . .]
  the lift isn't working no funciona el ascensor [noh foonth-*y*ona el ass-then*sor*]
light *(noun)* la luz [looth]
  the lights aren't working no funcionan las luces [noh foonth-*y*onan las *loo*thess]
  have you got a light? ¿tiene fuego? [tee-*eh*-neh fweh-goh]
  when it gets light cuando se haga de día [kwandoh seh *a*h-ga deh *dee*-a]
  light bulb una bombilla [–*bee*ya]
  (not heavy) ligero [lee-*h*eh-roh]
  light meter el fotómetro
like: would you like . . .? ¿quiere usted . . .? [kee-*eh*-reh oosteh]
  I'd like a . . ./I'd like to . . . quisiera un . . ./quisiera . . . [kees-*y*eh-ra]
  I like it/you me gusta/gustas [*goo*–]
  I don't like it no me gusta
  what's it like? ¿cómo es?
  do it like this hágalo así [*a*h-galoh ass*ee*]
  one like this uno como éste
lime lima [*lee*ma]
line línea [*lee*-neh-a]
lip el labio [*la*hb-yo]
  lipstick una barra de labios
  lip salve crema labial

liqueur un licor
» *TRAVEL TIP: Tia Maria: coffee liqueur; 43*
(kwarent-eye-tress): *orange like cointreau; anis:*
aniseed; Marie Brizard: anisette
liquidación *sale*
list *(noun)* una lista [leesta]
listen escuchar [eskoo–]
litre un litro [leetroh]
» *TRAVEL TIP: 1 litre = 1¾ pints = 0.22 gals*
little pequeño [peckehn-yoh]
  a little ice/a little more un poco de hielo/un
  poco más [. . . yeh-loh . . .]
  just a little sólo un poquito [poh-kee-toh]
live vivir [veeveer]; **I live in** . . . vivo en . . .
  where do you live? ¿dónde vive usted? [. . .
  veeveh oosteh]
liver el hígado [eegadoh]
lizard un lagarto
llegadas *arrivals*
loaf un pan
lobster langosta
local: could we try a local wine? ¿quisiéramos
  probar un vino de la localidad? [keess-yeh-
  ramoss pro-bar oon . . .]
  a local restaurant un restaurante del barrio
  [rest-ow-ranteh del barree-oh]
  is it made locally? ¿se fabrica aquí? [seh
  fabreeka akee]
lock: the lock's broken sa ha roto la cerradura
  [seh ah . . . therradoora]
  I've locked myself out no puedo entrar
  porque me he dejado la llave dentro [noh
  pweh-doh entrar porkeh meh eh deh-hadoh la
  yah-veh dentroh]
London Londres [londress]
lonely solitario [–tar-yoh]
long largo
  we'd like to stay longer nos gustaría
  quedarnos más tiempo [noss goostaree-a keh-
  darnoss mass tee-empoh]

....

that was long ago eso fue hace mucho tiempo
[. . . fweh *a*h-theh . . .]

longitude longitud [lon-*h*ee-t*oo*]

loo: where's the loo? ¿dónde está el wáter? [. .
v*a*tair]

look: you look tired parece usted cansado
[par*e*h-theh oost*e*h . . .]

I'm looking forward to . . . tengo muchas
ganas de . . .

I'm just looking sólo estoy mirando

I'm looking for . . . estoy buscando . . .

look at that mire eso [m*ee*-reh *e*h-soh]

look out! ¡cuidado! [kwee–]

loose suelto [sw*e*ll-toh]

lorry un camión [kam-y*on*]

lorry driver un camionero [kam-yon*e*h-roh]

lose perder [paird*ai*r]

I've lost my . . . he perdido mi . . . [eh
paird*ee*doh mee]

excuse me, I'm lost oiga, por favor, me he
perdido [*o*y-ga . . .]

lot: a lot/not a lot mucho/no mucho [m*oo*-choh
. . .]

a lot of chips/wine muchas patatas/
mucho vino

lots muchos

a lot more expensive mucho más caro

lotion una loción [loth-y*on*]

loud fuerte [fw*ai*rteh]

louder más fuerte

love: I love you te quiero [teh kee-*e*h-roh]

he's in love está enamorado

I love this wine me encanta este vino

do you love me? ¿me quieres? [meh kee-
*e*h-ress]

lovely encantad*o*r

low bajo [b*a*h-*h*oh]

luck suerte [sw*ai*r-teh]

good luck! ¡suerte!

lucky: you're lucky tiene suerte [tee-*e*h-neh
sw*ai*r-teh]

....

that's lucky! ¡qué suerte!
luggage equipaje [eckeh-pah-heh]
lumbago lumbago [loombah-goh]
lump un bulto [bool-toh]
lunch el almuerzo [al-mwair-thoh]
» *TRAVEL TIP: lunch normally available 1.30–3.30*
lungs los pulmones [pool-moh-ness]
luxurious lujoso [loo-hoh-soh]
luxury el lujo [loo-hoh]
 a luxury hotel un hotel de lujo
mad loco
madam señora [sen-yora]
made-to-measure hecho a la medida [etcho ah
 lah medeeda]
magazine una revista [–vee–]
magnificent magnífico
maiden name nombre de soltera [nombreh deh
 sol-teh-ra] *Spanish women retain their maiden
 name even when married*
mail correo
 is there any mail for me? ¿hay algún correo
 para mí? [eye algoon korreh-oh para mee]
mainland tierra firme [tee-erra feer-meh]
main road una calle principal [ka-yeh
 preentheepal]
 (in the country) la carretera principal
make hacer [athair]
 will we make it in time? ¿llegaremos a
 tiempo? [yeh-gareh-moss ah tee-empoh]
 make-up maquillaje [mackee-yah-heh]
man un hombre [ombreh]
manager el director [dee–]
 can I see the manager? quiero ver al director
 [kee-eh-roh vair . . .]
manicure manicura [–eekoo–]
manners modales [modah-less]
nany muchos [moochoss]
nap un mapa
 a map of . . . un mapa de . . . [. . . deh]
March marzo [–thoh]

....

margarine margarina
marina puerto deportivo [pw*ai*r-toh
deport*ee*voh]
mark: there's a mark on it tiene una mancha
[tee-*e*h-neh . . .]
market un merc*a*do [mair–]
marketplace el mercado
marmalade mermelada de naranja [mairmeh-
l*a*h-da deh nar*a*n-*h*a]
married casado
marry: will you marry me? ¿te quieres casar
conmigo? [teh kee-*e*h-ress kass*a*r konm*ee*goh]
marvellous maravilloso [–veey*o*h-soh]
mascara rímel
mashed potatoes puré de patatas [poor*e*h . . .]
massage masaje [mass*a*h-*h*eh]
mast el m*á*stil
mat una estera
match: a box of matches una caja de cerillas
[k*a*h-*h*a deh ther*ee*-yass]
football match un partido de f*ú*tbol [par-t*ee*
doh . . .]
material material [matteh-ree-*a*l]
(cloth) tejido [teh-*h*eedoh]
matter: it doesn't matter no importa
what's the matter? ¿qué ocurre? [keh
ok*oo*rreh]
mattress un colchón
mature maduro [–d*oo*–]
maximum máximo
May mayo [m*a*h-yoh]
may: may I have . . .? ¿me da . . .? [meh . . .]
maybe tal vez [. . . veth]
mayonnaise mayonesa [mah-yonn*e*h-sa]
me me [meh]
come with me venga conmigo [. . .–m*ee*goh]
it's for me es para mí [. . . mee]
it's me soy yo
meal una comida [komm*ee*da]
mean: what does this mean? ¿qué significa

esto? [keh signifeekah . . .]
by all means! ¡naturalmente!
[natooralmenteh]
measles sarampión [–yon]
German measles rubéola [roobeh-ola]
measurements medidas [–dee–]
meat carne [karneh]
mechanic: is there a mechanic here? ¿hay
algún mecánico aquí? [eye . . . akee]
medicine una medicina [–theena]
meet: pleased to meet you mucho gusto (en
conocerle) [moochoh goostoh (en konothair-
leh)]
when shall we meet? ¿cuándo nos reunimos?
[kwandoh noss reh-ooneemoss]
I met him in the street me encontré con él en
la calle [meh enkontreh . . . ka-yeh]
meeting una reunión [reh-oon-yon]
mellow *(wine)* suave [swah-veh]
melon un melón
member socio [soth-yoh]
how do I become a member? ¿cómo puedo
hacerme socio? [. . . pweh-doh athairmeh . . .]
men caballeros [kaba-yeh-ross]
mend: can you mend this? ¿puede arreglar
esto? [pweh-deh . . .]
mention: don't mention it de nada [deh . . .]
menu el menú [menoo]
can I have the menu, please? ¿me trae el
menú, por favor? [meh trah-eh . . .]
see pages 70–71
mess lío [lee-oh]
message: are there any messages for me?
¿hay algún recado para mí? [eye algoon reh-
kah-doh para mee]
can I leave a message for . . .? quisiera dejar
un recado para . . . [keess-yeh-ra deh-
har . . .]
metre un metro
» *TRAVEL TIP: 1 metre = 39.37 ins = 1.09 yds*

MENU

Starters
cocktail de gambas *prawn cocktail*
zumo de tomate *tomato juice*
espárragos con mayonesa *asparagus with
    mayonnaise*
ensaladilla Rusa *Russian salad*
ensalada mixta *mixed salad*
entremeses variados *mixed hors d'oeuvres*
croquetas *croquettes*

Sopas: Soup
gazpacho *refreshingly cold purée of tomato, bread,
    oil and vinegar + garlic and peppers*
consomé *clear soup*
sopa Juliana *shredded vegetable soup*
sopa sevillana *fish and mayonnaise*
crema de champiñones *cream of mushroom*
sopa de cebolla *onion with bread, cheese*

Verduras: Vegetable dishes
alcachofas salteadas con jamón *sautéed artichokes
    with ham*
menestra *stew of broad beans and other
    vegetables*
habas con jamón *broad beans fried with ham*

Carnes: Meat dishes
entrecot a la parrilla *grilled steak*
escalope Milanesa *escalope of veal fried in white
    sauce and bread-crumbs*
albóndigas *meatballs in sauce*
pierna de cordero *leg of lamb*
chuletas de cerdo *pork chops*
filete de ternera *beef steak*
lomo al ajillo *pork loin in garlic*

Aves y caza: Fowl and game
pollo asado *roast chicken*

gallina en pepitoria *chicken casserole with
  almonds, garlic etc*
pato a la naranja *duck in orange sauce*
perdiz/faisán/codorniz *partridge, pheasant, quail*

Pescado: Fish
merluza *hake*
mero *sea-bream*
lenguado *sole*
boquerones fritos *fresh anchovies fried*
calamares fritos *squid fried in batter*
calamares en su tinta *squid in its ink*
gambas a la plancha *grilled scampi*
pez espada *sword-fish*

Huevos: Egg dishes
tortilla española *potato omelette*
tortilla francesa *plain omelette*
tortilla de jamón *ham omelette*
huevos a la flamenca *eggs baked in tomato, ham,
  onion, asparagus, sausage*
huevos al plato *eggs baked in oven*
huevos fritos con jamón *fried eggs and gammon*
arroz a la cubana *fried eggs and banana with rice
  and tomato purée*

Others
paella *rice, shellfish, meat, peas, tomato, red
  peppers and saffron*
fabada asturiana *butter-bean stew*
cocido *chick-pea stew, sausage and veg.*

Postres: Desserts
fruta del tiempo *seasonal fruit*
piña *pineapple*
melocotón en almíbar *peach in syrup*
flan *caramel custard*
tarta helada *multi-layered ice-cream*
pijama *caramel custard, ice-cream, fruit
  and syrup*

....

metro *underground*
midday mediodía [mehd-yoh-d*ee*-a]
middle: in the middle en el centro [th–]
  in the middle of the road en medio de la calle
  [en m*e*hd-yoh . . . k*a*-yeh]
midnight medianoche [meh-dee-ah-n*o*tcheh]
might: I might be late es posible que llegue
  tarde [ess poss*ee*bleh keh y*e*h-gheh t*a*rdeh]
  he might have gone es posible que se haya ido
  [. . . seh *a*h-ya *ee*-doh]
migraine jaqueca [*h*ackeh-ka]
mild suave [sw*a*h-veh]
  (weather) templado
mile una milla [m*ee*-ya]
»*TRAVEL TIP: conversion:* $\dfrac{miles}{5} \times 8 = kilometres$

miles	$\frac{1}{2}$	1	3	5	10	50	100
kilometres	0.8	1.6	4.8	8	16	80	160

milk leche [l*e*h-cheh]
  a glass of milk un vaso de leche [b*a*h-soh
  deh . . .]
  milkshake un batido [–t*ee*–]
millimetre un mil*í*metro
millionaire millonario [mee-yon*a*r-yoh]
milometer el cuentakil*ó*metros [kw*e*nta . . .]
minced meat carne picada [k*a*rneh . . .]
mind: I've changed my mind he cambiado de
  idea [eh kamb-y*a*-doh deh eed*e*h-a]
  I don't mind me es igual [meh ess eeg-w*a*l]
  do you mind if I . . .? ¿le importa si . . .?
  [leh . . .]
  never mind ¡qué más da! [keh . . .]
mine mío [m*ee*-oh]
  it's mine es mío
mineral water agua mineral [*a*hg-wa meeneh-
  r*a*l]
minimum m*í*nimo
minus menos [m*e*h-noss]
  minus 3 degrees tres grados bajo cero [. . .
  b*a*h-*h*oh th*e*h-roh]

minute un minuto [–een*oo*–]
  in a minute en seguida [segh*ee*-da]
  just a minute un momento
mirror un espejo [essp*e*h-*h*oh]
Miss Señorita [sen-yor*ee*ta]
miss: **I miss you** le echo de menos [leh *e*tchoh
  deh m*e*h-noss]
  he is missing falta
  there is a . . . missing falta un/una . . .
mist bruma [br*oo*ma]
mistake una equivocación [eckeevoh-kath-yon]
  I think you've made a mistake me parece
  que se ha equivocado usted [meh par*e*h-theh
  keh seh ah eckeevok*a*h-doh oost*e*h]
misunderstanding un malentendido
modern moderno [–d*ai*r–]
Monday lunes [l*oo*ness]
money dinero [dee-n*e*h-roh]
  I've lost my money se me ha perdido el dinero
  [seh meh ah paird*ee*doh . . .]
  I've no money no tengo dinero
  »*TRAVEL TIP: see* **change**
month un mes [mess]
moon la luna [l*oo*–]
moorings el amarradero
moped un ciclomotor [theekloh–]
more más
  can I have some more? ¿me da un poco más?
  [meh . . .]
  more wine, please más vino, por favor
  no more ya no más
  more comfortable más cómodo
  more than three/that más de tres/que eso
  [. . . deh . . ./keh . . .]
morning la mañana [man-y*a*h-na]
  good morning buenos días [bw*e*h-noss dee-
  ass]
  this morning esta mañana
  in the morning por la mañana
mosquito un mosquito

....

most: I like it/you the most es el que más me
gusta/eres quien más me gusta [. . . el keh . . ./
eh-ress kee-*en* . . .]
most of the time/the people la mayor parte
del tiempo/la mayoría de la gente [ma-yor
parteh del tee-*em*po/ma-yor*ee*-a . . . . *hen*teh]
that's most kind muy amable de su parte
[mwee am*a*h-bleh deh soo p*a*rteh]
motel un motel
mother: my mother mi madre [mee m*a*h-dreh]
motor el mot*o*r
motorbike una moto
motorboat una motora
motor cyclist un motorista [–ree–]
motorist un automovilista [ow-tomovee*lee*sta]
motorway autopista [ow-top*ee*sta]
mountain una montaña [mont*a*h-ya]
mouse un ratón
moustache bigote [beeg*o*teh]
mouth la boca
move: don't move no se mueva [no seh
mweh-va]
could you move your car? ¿podría usted
cambiar de sitio su coche? [podr*ee*-a oost*e*h
kamb-y*a*r deh s*ee*t-yo soo k*o*tcheh]
Mr Señor
Mrs Señora [sen-y*o*ra]
Ms *no exact equivalent in Spanish*
much mucho [m*oo*tchoh]
much better/much more mucho mejor/
mucho más [. . . meh-*ho*r]
not much no mucho
mug: I've been mugged me han atacado [meh
an . . .]
mum mam*á*
muscle un músculo [–*oo*skoo–]
museum un museo [moos*e*h-oh]
mushrooms champiñones [champeen-yoh-ness]
music música [m*oo*sseeka]
must: I must have . . . tengo que tom*a*r . . .

I must not eat . . . no debo comer . . . [noh deh-boh komair]
you must (do it) debe usted de hacerlo [deh-beh oosteh deh athair-loh]
must I . . .? ¿tengo que . . .? [. . . keh]
mustard mostaza [mosstah-tha]
my mi [mee]
nail *(finger)* una uña [oon-ya]
(wood) un clavo
nailfile una lima para las uñas [leema . . .]
nail polish esmalte para las uñas [ezmal-teh . . .]
nail clippers un cortauñas [korta-oon-yass]
nail scissors unas tijeritas de uñas [tee-heh-reetass . . .]
naked desnudo [dess-noodoh]
name el nombre [–breh]
my name is . . . me llamo . . . [meh yah-moh]
what's your name? ¿cómo se llama usted? [. . . seh yah-ma oosteh]
napkin una servilleta [sairvee-yeh-ta]
nappy un pañal [pan-yal]
narrow estrecho
national nacional [nath-yonal]
nationality la nacionalidad
natural natural [–too–]
naughty: don't be naughty! ¡no seas malo! [. . . seh-ass . . .]
near: is it near? ¿está cerca? [. . . thair-ka]
near here cerca de aquí [. . . akee]
do you go near . . .? ¿va a pasar usted cerca de . . .? [. . . oosteh . . .]
where is the nearest . . .? ¿dónde está el . . . más cercano? [. . . thair-kah-noh]
nearly casi [kah-see]
neat *(drink)* solo
necessary necesario [nethessar-yoh]
it's not necessary no es necesario
neck el cuello [kweh-yoh]
necklace un collar [koy-yar]

....

need: I need a ... necesito un ...
  [nethess*ee*toh]
needle una aguja [ag*oo*-*h*a]
negotiation negociación [negoth-yath-yon]
neighbour vecino [veth*ee*noh]
neither: neither of them ninguno de los dos
  [neeng*oo*noh ...]
  neither ... nor ... ni ... ni ... [nee ...]
  neither do I ni yo tampoco
nephew: my nephew mi sobrino [mee
  sobr*ee*noh]
nervous nervioso [nairv-yosoh]
net una red [reth]
  net price precio neto [pr*e*th-yoh n*e*h-toh]
never nunca; **well I never!** ¡caramba!
new nuevo [nweh-voh]
  New Year Año Nuevo [an-yoh]
  New Year's Eve Nochevieja [notcheh vee-
  eh-*h*a]
  Happy New Year Feliz Año Nuevo [feh-
  l*ee*th ...]
  *In Spain it is traditional to swallow one grape or
  each stroke of midnight*
news noticias [noh-t*ee*th-yass]
  newsagent's una tienda de periódicos [tee-
  enda deh peh-ree-oddeekoss]
  newspaper un periódico
  do you have any English newspapers?
  ¿tiene usted algún periódico inglés? [tee-eh-neh
  oosteh alg*oo*n peh-ree-oddeekoh eengl*e*ss]
New Zealand Nueva Zelanda [nweh-va theh-
  l*a*nda]
New Zealander neozelandés
  [neh-o-theh-land*e*ss]
next próximo
  sit next to me siéntese a mi lado [see-enteh
  seh ...]
  please stop at the next corner haga el favor
  de parar en la esquina próxima [ah-ga ...
  esk*ee*na ...]

see you next year hasta el año que viene [asta el an-yoh keh vee-eh-neh]
next week/next Tuesday la semana/el martes que viene
nice agradable [–dah-bleh]
niece: my niece mi sobrina [mee sobreena]
night noche [notcheh]
  goodnight buenas noches [bweh-nass notchess]
  at night por la noche
  is there a good night club here? ¿dónde hay un buen 'night club'? [dondeh eye oon bwen . . .]
  night-life vida nocturna [veeda noctoorna]
  night porter el portero [porteh-roh]
no no
  there's no water no hay agua [noh eye ahg-wa]
  no way! ¡de ninguna manera! [. . . maneh-ra]
  I've no money no tengo dinero [deeneh-roh]
no potable *not for drinking*
nobody nadie [nahd-yeh]
  nobody saw it nadie lo vió [. . . vee-oh]
noisy ruidoso [rweedosoh]
  our room is too noisy se oye demasiado ruido en nuestra habitación [seh o-yeh demass-yah-doh rweedoh en nwestra abbee-tath-yon]
none ninguno
  none of them ninguno de ellos [neengoonoh deh eh-yoss]
nonsense tonterías [–ree-ass]
normal normal
north norte [–teh]
Northern Ireland Irlanda del Norte [. . . norteh]
nose la nariz [–eeth]; **nosebleed** una hemorragia nasal [emmorah-hee-ah nassal]
not no
  I'm not hungry no tengo hambre [. . . ambreh]

....

not that one ese no [eh-seh . . .]
not me yo no
I don't understand no entiendo [. . . ent-
yendoh]
he didn't tell me no me lo dijo [. . . meh loh
dee-hoh]
note *(bank note)* un billete [bee-yeh-teh]
nothing nada
November noviembre [novee-embreh]
now ahora [ah-ora]
nowhere en ningún sitio [en neengoon seet-yoh]
nudist nudista [noodeesta]
   nudist beach una playa nudista [plah-ya . . .]
nuisance: it's a nuisance es una lata
   this man is being a nuisance este hombre me
   está molestando [. . . ombreh meh . . .]
numb entumecido [entoomeh-theedoh]
number un número [noo–]
   number plate la placa de la matrícula
   [–eekoo–] *see pages 127–128*
nurse una enfermera [emfair-meh-ra]
nursery slope la pista de principiantes [peesta
   deh preen-theep-yantess]
nut una nuez [nweth]
   (for bolt) una tuerca [twairka]
oar un remo [reh-moh]
objetos perdidos *lost property*
obligatory obligatorio [obleegator-yoh]
obras *roadworks*
obviously evidentemente [–teh]
occasionally de vez en cuando [deh veth en
   kwandoh]
occupied ocupado
o'clock *see* time
October octubre [oktoobreh]
octopus un pulpo [pool]
ocupado *engaged*
odd *(number)* impar [eem–]
   (strange) raro [rah–]
of de [deh]

off: the milk/meat is off la leche está
  cortada/la carne está pasada [. . . leh-cheh
  . . ./. . . karneh . . .]
  it just came off se ha soltado sin más [seh
  ah . . .]
  10% off un descuento del diez por ciento [oon
  dess-kwentoh del dee-eth por thee-entoh]
offence un insulto [eensooltoh]
  (legal) una infracción [eemfrakth-yon]
office la oficina [–eethee–]
officer *(to policeman)* agente [ahenteh]
official *(noun)* un funcionario [foonth-yonah-
  ree-oh]
often a menudo [ah menoodoh]
oil aceite [athay-teh]
  I'm losing oil estoy perdiendo aceite [. . .
  pairdee-endoh . . .]
  will you change the oil? ¿quiere cambiar el
  aceite? [kee-eh-reh kamb-yar . . .]
ointment pomada
OK! ¡vale! [bah-leh]
old viejo [vee-eh-hoh]
  how old are you? ¿cuántos años tienes?
  [kwantoss an-yoss tee-eh-ness]
olive una aceituna [athay-toona]
  olive oil aceite de oliva [athay-teh deh oleeva]
omelette una tortilla [torteeya]
on en
  I haven't got it on me no lo llevo encima
  [. . . yeh-vo enthee-ma]
  on Friday el viernes [. . . vee-airness]
  on television en la tele [. . . teh-leh]
once una vez [veth]
  at once en seguida [seh-gheeda]
one uno [oono]
  the red one el rojo [ro-ho]
onion una cebolla [theh-boy-ya]
only *(adjective)* único [ooneekoh]
  only one sólo uno
  only once sólo una vez [. . . veth]

....

open *(adjective)* abierto [ab-y*a*irtoh]
  I can't open it no puedo abrirlo [noh pw*e*h-doh abr*e*erloh] **when do you open?** ¿a qué hora abre? [ah keh *o*ra *a*h-breh]
opera la ópera
operation una operación [–ath-yon]
  will I need an operation? ¿necesitaré una operación? [nethesseetar*e*h . . .]
operator *(tel)* la operadora
» *TRAVEL TIP: dial 009 (national) or 008 (international)*
opposite: opposite the hotel enfrente del hotel [emfr*e*nteh del o-t*e*l]
optician's una óptica
or o
orange naranja [nar*a*n-*h*a]
  orange juice zumo de naranja [th*oo*-moh . . .]
order: could we order now? ¿podemos pedir ya la comida? [pod*e*h-moss ped*e*er ya la kom*ee*da]
  thank you, we've already ordered gracias, ya hemos pedido [. . . yah *e*h-moss ped*ee*doh]
other: the other one el otro
  do you have any others? ¿tiene usted más de estos? [tee-*e*h-neh oost*e*h . . .]
  (different ones) ¿tiene usted otros distintos?
otherwise de otra manera
ought: I ought to go debería irme [deber*ee*-a *e*er-meh]
ounce una onza [*o*ntha]
» *TRAVEL TIP: 1 ounce = 28.35 grammes*
our nuestro [nw*e*sstroh]
  that's ours eso es nuestro
out: we're out of petrol se nos ha acabado la gasolina [seh noss ah . . .]
  get out! ¡fuera! [fw*e*h-ra]
outboard *(motor)* fuera-bordo
outdoors fuera de casa
outside: can we sit outside? ¿podemos sentarnos fuera? [pod*e*h-moss . . .]

over: over here/there aquí/allá [akee/a-ya]
  over 40 más de cuarenta [. . . kwarenta]
  it's all over ¡se acabó!
overboard: man overboard! ¡hombre al agua!
  [ombreh al ahg-wa]
overcharge: you've overcharged me me ha
  cobrado de más [meh ah . . .]
overcooked recocido [reh-kotheedoh]
overexposed sobreexpuesto [soh-breh-
  esspwessto]
overnight *(travel)* durante la noche [doo–. . .]
oversleep dormir demasiado [dormeer demass-
  yah-doh]
  I overslept se me han pegado las sábanas [seh
  meh an . . .]
overtake adelantar
owe: what do I owe you? ¿cuánto le debo?
  [kwantoh leh dehboh]
own *(adjective)* propio [proh-pee-oh]
  my own . . . mi propio . . .
  I'm on my own estoy solo
owner el propietario [proh-pee-eh-tar-yoh]
oxygen oxígeno [oxee-heh-noh]
oyster una ostra
pack: I haven't packed yet todavía no he
  hecho las maletas [tohda-vee-a noh eh
  etchoh . . .]
  can I have a packed lunch? ¿me puede poner
  la comida en bocadillos? [meh pweh-deh ponair
  la komeeda en bokadee-yoss]
  package tour un viaje organizado [oom bee-
  ah-heh organeethah-doh]
page *(of book)* página [pah-heena]
  could you page him? ¿podría llamarle por los
  altavoces? [podree-a yamarleh por loss
  altavothess]
pain dolor
  I've got a pain in my . . . me duele el . . .
  [meh dweh-leh . . .]
  painkillers calmantes [kalmantess]

....

painting un cuadro [kwadroh]
Pakistan Paquistán
Pakistani paquistaní
pale pálido
pancake una crêpe [krep]
panties las bragas
pants los pantalones [–o-ness]
  (underpants) los calzoncillos [kalthon-theeyoss]
paper papel
  (newspaper) un periódico [peh-ree-oddeekoh]
parada stop (bus etc)
paraffin parafina [–fee–]
parcel un paquete [pakeh-teh]
pardon? *(didn't understand)* ¿cómo?
  I beg your pardon *(sorry)* usted perdone
  [oosteh pairdoh-neh]
parents: my parents mis padres [meess pahdress]
park el parque [parkeh]
  where can I park my car? ¿dónde puedo
  aparcar el coche? [dondeh pweh-doh . . .
  kotcheh]
part una parte [–teh]
partner pareja [pareh-ha]
party *(group)* un grupo [groo–]
  (celebration) una fiesta
  I'm with the . . . party estoy en el grupo de . . .
pasen cross
paso a nivel level crossing
pass *(mountain)* un puerto [pwairtoh]
  he's passed out ha perdido el conocimiento
  [ah pairdeedoh el konotheem-yentoh]
passable *(road)* transitable [–eetah-bleh]
passenger un pasajero [passa-heh-roh]
passer-by un transeúnte [tran-seh-oonteh]
passport pasaporte [passaporteh]
past: in the past antiguamente [anteegwamenteh]
pastry masa
  (cakes) pastelillos [pastel-eeyoss]

path un camino [−m*ee*−]
patient: be patient tenga paciencia [. . . path-yenth-ya]
pattern *(on cloth, etc)* dibujo [dee-boo-*h*oh]
pavement la acera [ath*eh*-ra]
pay pag*a*r
  can I pay, please? ¿me puede cobr*a*r, por favor? [meh pweh-deh . . .]
» *TRAVEL TIP: it's usual to pay when you leave not when you order*
peace paz [path]
peach un melocotón
peaje *toll*
peanut un cacahuete [kacka-w*eh*-teh]
pear una pera [p*eh*-ra]
peas guisantes [ghee-s*a*ntess]
peatones *pedestrians*
pebble un guijarro [ghee-*h*arroh]
pedal *(noun)* un ped*a*l
pedestrian un peatón [peh-ah-t*o*nn]
  pedestrian crossing un paso de peat*o*nes [−ness]
» *TRAVEL TIP: beware! cars don't always stop*
peg una pinza [p*ee*n-tha]
  (camping) una estaca
peligro *danger*
peligro de incendio *danger of fire*
pelvis la pelvis [−*ee*ss]
pen una pluma [pl*oo*ma]
  have you got a pen? ¿tiene un bolígrafo? [tee-*e*h-neh oon bol*ee*grafoh]
pencil un lápiz [l*a*peeth]
pen friend amigo por correspondencia [. . . −d*e*nth-ya]
penicillin penicilina [peneethee*lee*na]
penknife una navaja [navah-*h*a]
pensioner un pensionista [penss-yon*ee*sta]
people gente [*h*enteh]
  the Spanish people los españoles [esspan-y*o*less]

....

pepper *(spice)* pimienta [peem-yenta]
  (vegetable) pimiento
peppermint menta
per: per night/week/person por noche/
  semana/persona
per cent por ciento [. . . thee-entoh]
perfect perfecto [pair–]
  the perfect holiday las vacaciones perfectas
  [vakath-yoness]
perfume perfume [pairfoomeh]
perhaps quizás [keethass]
period *(also medical)* el período [peh-ree-odoh]
perm una permanente [pairmanenteh]
permit *(noun)* un permiso [pair-meesoh]
person una persona [pair–]
  in person en persona
petrol gasolina [–eena]
  petrol station una gasolinera
» *TRAVEL TIP: extra = 4 star; super = 3 star;*
  normal = 2 star
phone *see* **telephone**
photograph una foto
  would you take a photograph of us? ¿le
  importaría hacernos una foto? [leh
  eemportaree-ah athair-noss . . .]
piano un piano
pickpocket un ratero
pie una empanada
  (fruit) una tarta
piece un pedazo [pedah-thoh]
  a piece of . . . un pedazo de . . .
pig un cerdo [thair-doh]
pigeon una paloma
pile-up un accidente múltiple [ak-theedenteh
  moolteepleh]
pill una píldora
  do you take the pill? ¿toma la píldora?
pillion *(passenger)* el pasajero de atrás [passa-
  heh-roh . . .]; **on the pillion** en el asiento de
  atrás [. . . ass-yentoh . . .]

pillow una almohada [almoh-*a*h-da]
pin un alfiler [alfee-l*ai*r]
pineapple piña [p*ee*n-ya]
pint una pinta [p*ee*nta]
» *TRAVEL TIP: 1 pint = 0.57 litres*
pipe una pipa [p*ee*pa]
  pipe tobacco tabaco de pipa
piso *floor*
piston un pistón
pity: it's a pity es una lástima
place un sitio [s*ee*t-yoh]
  is this place taken? ¿está ocupado este sitio?
  do you know any good places to go? ¿sabe de sitios buenos adonde ir? [s*a*h-beh . . . bweh-noss ad*o*ndeh eer]
plain *(food)* sencilla [sen-th*ee*ya]
  (not patterned) liso [l*ee*-soh]
plane un avión [av-yon]
plant una planta
plaster *(medical)* escayola
  see **sticking**
plastic plástico
plate un plato
platform el andén
  which platform, please? ¿qué andén, por favor? [keh . . .]
play: *(verb)* jugar [h*oo*gar]
pleasant agradable [–d*a*h-bleh]
please: could you please . . .? ¿podría hacer el favor de . . .? [podr*ee*-ah ath*ai*r . . .]
  (yes) please por favor
pleasure placer [plath-*ai*r]
  it's my pleasure no hay de qué [no eye deh keh]
plenty: plenty of . . . mucho . . . [moo–]
  thank you, that's plenty ya basta, gracias
pliers unos alicates [–*a*h-tess]
plimsolls unas zapatillas de deporte [thapat*ee*-yass deh deh-p*o*rteh]
plonk vino

....

plug *(elec)* un enchufe [ench*oo*feh]
  (car) una bujía [boo-*hee*-a]
  (bathroom) el tapón
» *TRAVEL TIP: you'll need 2-pin plugs in Spain*
plum una ciruela [theer-w*e*h-la]
plumber el fontanero
plus más
p.m. de la tarde *see* **a.m.**
pneumonia neumonía [neh-oo-mon*ee*-a]
poached egg un huevo escalfado [w*e*h-voh . . .]
pocket un bolsillo [bols*ee*-yoh]
point: could you point to it? ¿puede señalarlo?
  [pw*e*h-deh senyal*a*rloh]
  four point six cuatro coma seis [kw*a*troh
  k*o*ma sayss]
  points *(car)* los platinos [–*tee*–]
police la policía [–*thee*-a]
  get the police llame a la policía [y*a*h-meh . . .]
  policeman un policía
  police station la comisaría [–*ree*-a]
» *TRAVEL TIP: dial 091; the national police wear a
  brown uniform with a beret*
polish *(noun)* betún [–*toon*]
  will you polish my shoes? ¿quiere limpiarme
  los zapatos? [kee-*e*h-reh leemp-y*a*rmeh loss
  thap*a*h-toss]
» *TRAVEL TIP: you can have your shoes cleaned in
  the street by travelling 'limpiabotas'*
polite fino [f*ee*noh]
politics la política [–*lee*–]
polluted contaminado
polythene bag una bolsa de plástico
pool *(swimming)* una piscina [peess-th*ee*na]
poor: I'm very poor soy muy pobre [. . . mw*ee*
  p*o*h-breh]
  poor quality de baja calidad [b*a*h-h*a* . . .]
popular popul*a*r [–*poo*–]
population la población [–*a*th-yon]
pork carne de cerdo [k*a*r-neh deh th*a*ir-doh]
port un puerto [pw*a*irtoh]

....

(drink) un Oporto
to port a babor
porter el conserje [kon-sair-*h*eh]
(for luggage) un mozo [moh-thoh]
portrait un retrato
posh *(restaurant)* de lujo [loo-*h*oh]
(people) snob [essnob]
possible posible [poss*ee*bleh]
could you possibly . . .? ¿le sería posible . . .?
[leh ser*ee*-ah . . .]
post *(noun)* correo [korreh-oh]
  postbox un buzón [booth*on*]
  postcard una post*al*
  post office la oficina de Correos [offee-
  theena . . .]
» *TRAVEL TIP: look for the sign 'correos'; letter boxes
are yellow; letters for abroad in slit marked
'extranjero'; see stamps*
poste restante la lista de Correos [l*ee*sta deh
korreh-oss]
potato una patata
pottery cerámica [th–]
pound *(weight, money)* una libra [l*ee*bra]
» *TRAVEL TIP: conversion:* $\dfrac{pounds}{11} \times 5 = kilos$

pounds	1	3	5	6	7	8	9
kilos	0.45	1.4	2.3	2.7	3.2	3.6	4.1

pour: it's pouring está lloviendo a cántaros
[yov-yendoh . . .]
powder polvo
(face) polvos para la cara
power cut un apagón
power point una toma de corriente [. . . korr-
yenteh]
prawns gambas
  prawn cocktail un cocktail de gambas
precaución caution
prefer: I prefer this one prefiero éste [pref-
yeh-roh essteh]
pregnant embarazada [–ath*a*h-da]

....

prescription una receta [reh-theh-ta]
present: at present actualmente [aktwal-menteh]
  present company excepted mejorando lo presente [meh-horandoh lo press-enteh]
  here's a present for you le traigo un regalo [leh try-goh oon regah-loh]
president el presidente [–teh]
press: could you press these? ¿puede plancharmelos? [pweh-deh . . . –meh-loss]
pretty mono
  it's pretty good es bastante bueno [. . . bweh-noh]
price el precio [preth-yoh]
priest un sacerdote [sathair-doteh]
principio de autopista start of motorway
printed matter impresos
prioridad a la derecha priority to the right
prison la cárcel [–thel]
private privado
probably probablemente [probah-bleh-menteh]
problem un problema
product un producto [–doo–]
profit una ganancia [gananth-ya]
prohibido forbidden
  prohibido adelantar no overtaking
  prohibido aparcar no parking
  prohibido el paso no trespassing
  prohibido fumar no smoking
promise: do you promise? ¿lo promete? [pro-meh-teh]
  I promise lo prometo
pronounce: how do you pronounce this? ¿cómo se pronuncia esto? [. . . pronoonth-ya . . .]
propeller una hélice [ellee-theh]
properly correctamente [–teh]
property propiedad [proh-pee-eh-da]
prostitute una prostituta [–toota]
protect proteger [pro-teh-hair]

Protestant protestante [–teh]
proud orgulloso [orgoo-yosoh]
prove: I can prove it puedo probarlo [pweh-doh . . .]
public: the public el público [poo–]
  public convenience aseos públicos [ass-eh-oss . . .]
» *TRAVEL TIP: see* **toilet**
» *TRAVEL TIP: public holidays*
  Jan 1 Año Nuevo *New Year's Day*
  Jan 6 Día de Reyes *Epiphany*
  Mar 19 San José *Saint Joseph*
          Viernes Santo *Good Friday*
          Lunes de Pascua *Easter Monday*
  May 1 Día del Trabajo *Labour Day*
          Corpus Christi *Corpus Christi*
  Jun 24 Onomástica del Rey *King's St. Day*
  Jul 25 Día de Santiago *Saint James*
  Aug 15 Día de la Asunción *Assumption*
  Oct 12 Día de la Hispanidad *Columbus Day*
  Nov 1 Todos los Santos *All Saints Day*
  Dec 8 Inmaculada Concepción *Immaculate Conception*
  Dec 25 Navidad *Christmas*
pudding pudín [poodeen]
pull *(verb)* tirar de [tee–]
  he pulled out in front of me salió delante de mí sin mirar [sal-yoh deh-lanteh deh mee seen meerar]
pump la bomba
punctual puntual [poont-wal]
puncture un pinchazo [peen-cha-thoh]
pure puro [pooroh]
purple púrpura [poor-poora]
purse el monedero
push *(verb)* empujar [empoo-har]
  push-chair una sillita de ruedas [see-yeeta deh rweh-dass]
put: where can I put . . .? ¿dónde puedo poner . . .? [dondeh pweh-doh pon-air]

....

where have you put ...? ¿dónde ha
puesto ...? [... ah pwesstoh]
pyjamas el pijama [pee-*ha*-ma]
quality calidad [–d*a*]
quarantine cuarentena [kwarent*e*h-na]
quarter la cuarta parte [kw*a*rta p*a*rteh]
  a quarter of an hour un cuarto de hora
  [kw*a*rtoh deh *o*ra]
quay el muelle [mw*e*h-yeh]
question una pregunta [–g*oo*–]
queue *(noun)* una cola
» *TRAVEL TIP: don't expect orderly queueing as in*
UK
quick rápido; **that was quick** sí que ha sido
rápido [see keh ah s*ee*doh ...]
quiet tranquilo [–k*ee*loh]
  be quiet! ¡cállese! [k*a*-yeh-seh]
quite *(fairly)* bastante [–teh]
  (very) completamente [–teh]
  quite a lot bastante
race *(sport: noun)* una carrera
radiator el radiador [radd*ee*ah–]
radio la radio [r*a*hd-yoh]
rail: by rail en tren
rain la lluvia [y*oo*v-ya]
  it's raining está lloviendo [... yov-y*e*ndoh]
  raincoat un impermeable [eem-pair-meh-
  *a*h-bleh]
rally *(car)* rallye
rape una violación [vee-olath-y*o*n]
rare poco común [... kom*oo*n]
  (steak) poco hecho [... *e*tchoh]
raspberry frambuesa [fram-bw*e*h-sa]
rat una rata
rather: I'd rather sit here prefiero sentarme
aquí [pref-y*e*h-roh sent*a*rmeh ak*ee*]
  I'd rather not prefiero no hacerlo [...
  ath*ai*r-loh]
  it's rather hot hace bastante calor [*a*h-
  theh ...]

raw crudo [kroodoh]

razor una maquinilla de afeitar [mackee-nee-ya deh affay-tar]

    razor blades hojas de afeitar [o-hass . . .]

read: **you read it** léalo usted [leh-ah-loh oosteh]

    something to read algo para leer [. . . leh-air]

ready: **when will it be ready?** ¿cuándo estará listo? [kwandoh estara leestoh]

    I'm not ready yet aún no estoy listo [ah-oon noh esstoy leestoh]

real verdadero [vair-da-deh-roh]

really realmente [reh-al-menteh]

rear-view mirror el (espejo) retrovisor [esspeh-hoh retroh-veesor]

reasonable razonable [rathonah-bleh]

rebajas *sale*

receipt un recibo [rethee-boh]

    can I have a receipt, please? por favor, ¿me da un recibo?

recently recientemente [reth-yenteh-menteh]

reception *(hotel)* Recepción [rethepth-yon]

    at reception en Recepción

receptionist recepcionista [–eesta]

recién pintado *wet paint*

recipe una receta [retheh-ta]

recommend: **can you recommend . . .?** ¿puede usted recomendar . . .? [pweh-deh oosteh . . .]

record *(music)* un disco [dee–]

red rojo [roh-hoh]

reduction un descuento [dess-kwentoh]

refuse: **I refuse** me niego [meh nee-eh-goh]

region una zona [tho-na]

registered letter una carta certificada [. . . thair-teefeekah-da]

regret: **I have no regrets** no me arrepiento [noh meh arrep-yentoh]

relax: **I just want to relax** sólo quiero descansar [. . . kee-eh-roh . . .]

    relax! ¡tranquilo! [tran-keeloh]

....

remember: don't you remember? ¿no se acuerda usted? [noh seh akwairda oosteh]

I'll always remember siempre (lo) recordaré [see-empreh reh-korda-reh]

something to remember you by algún recuerdo suyo [algoon reh-kwairdoh sooyoh]

RENFE = Red Nacional de Ferrocarriles Españoles National Railway

rent: can I rent a car/boat/bicycle? ¿puedo alquilar un coche/un barco/una bicicleta? [pweh-doh alkeelar oon kotcheh/. . . beetheekleh-ta]

repair: can you repair it? ¿puede arreglarlo? [pweh-deh . . .]

repeat: could you repeat that? ¿puede repetir eso? [pweh-deh reh-peteer . . .]

reputation fama [fah-ma]

rescue *(verb)* rescatar

reservation una reserva [–sair–]

I want to make a reservation for . . . quiero hacer una reserva para . . . [kee-eh-roh ath-air . . .]

reserve: can I reserve a seat? ¿puedo reservar un asiento? [pweh-doh reh-sair-var oon ass-yentoh]

responsible responsable [–sah-bleh]

rest: I've come here for a rest he venido aquí para descansar [eh veneedoh akee . . .]

you keep the rest quédese con la diferencia [keh-deh-seh kon la deeferenth-ya]

restaurant un restaurante [rest-ow-ranteh]

retail price el precio de venta [preth-yoh . . .]

retired jubilado [hoobeelah-doh]

retrete toilet

return: a return/two returns to . . . un billete/dos billetes de ida y vuelta a . . . [. . . beeyeh-teh . . . deh eeda ee vwelta]

reverse gear la marcha atrás

rheumatism reúma [reh-ooma]

rib una costilla [kosteeya]

rice arroz [arroth]
rich rico [reekoh]
(cake) empalagoso
ridiculous ridículo [reedeekooloh]
right: that's right eso es
  you're right tiene usted razón [tee-eh-neh
  oosteh rathon]
  on the right a la derecha
  right now ahora mismo [ah-orah meez-moh]
  right here aquí mismo [akee . . .]
  right-hand drive con el volante a la derecha
  [. . . volanteh . . .]
ring *(on finger)* una sortija [sor-tee-ha]
ripe maduro [–doo–]
rip-off: it's a rip-off es un timo [. . . teemoh]
river un río [ree-oh]
road la carretera
  which is the road to . . .? ¿cuál es la carretera
  de . . .? [kwal ess la karreteh-ra deh]
  roadhog un loco del volante [. . . –teh]
rob: I've been robbed! ¡me han robado! [meh
  an . . .]
rock *(noun)* una roca
  whisky on the rocks whisky con hielo
  [. . yeh-loh]
roll *(bread)* un panecillo [paneh-theeyoh]
Roman Catholic católico
romantic romántico
roof el tejado [tehah-doh]
room la habitación [abee-tath-yon]
  have you got a single/double room? ¿tiene
  una habitación individual/doble? [tee-eh-
  neh . . . eendeeveed-wal/dobleh]
  for one night/for three nights para una
  noche/para tres noches [. . . notcheh . . .]
  YOU MAY THEN HEAR . . .
  lo siento, está lleno [loh see-entoh, esta yeh-
  noh] *sorry, we're full up*
room service servicio de habitaciones [sair-
  veeth-yoh deh abbee-tath-yoness]

....

rope una cuerda [kwair-da]

rose una rosa [roh-sa]

rough *(sea, weather)* revuelto [reh-vwel-toh]

roughly *(approximately)* aproximadamente [–teh]

roulette la ruleta [rooleh-ta]

round *(circular)* redondo

roundabout *(traffic)* un cruce en glorieta [kroo-theh en glor-yeh-ta]

route una ruta [roota]
   which is the prettiest/fastest route? ¿cuál es la ruta más bonita/más rápida? [kwal . . .]

rowing boat un barco de remos [. . . reh-moss]

rubber goma
   rubber band una goma elástica

rubbish *(garbage)* basura [–soo–]
   it's rubbish no vale nada [. . . vah-leh . . .]
   rubbish! ¡tonterías! [tonteh-ree-ass]

rucksack una mochila [–chee–]

rudder el timón

rude grosero [groh-seh-roh]
   (indecent) indecente [eendeh-thenteh]

ruin *(noun)* una ruina [rweena]

rum ron
   rum and coke un Cubalibre de ron [koobaleebreh deh . . .]

run: hurry, run! ¡corra, dese prisa! [. . . deh-seh pree-sa]
   I've run out of petrol/money se me ha acabado la gasolina/el dinero [seh meh ah ackabah-doh . . .]

sad triste [treess-teh]

safe seguro [–goo–]
   will it be safe here? ¿estará seguro aquí [. . . akee]
   is it safe to swim here? ¿se puede nadar sin peligro aquí? [seh pweh-deh nadar seen peleegroh akee]

safety seguridad [segooreeda]
   safety pin un imperdible [eem-pair-deebleh]

sail una vela [veh-la]
  can we go sailing? ¿podemos hacer vela?
  [podeh-moss ath-air . . .]
sailor un marinero [maree-neh-roh]
  (sport) un marino
sala de espera waiting room
salad la ensalada
saldos sale
sale: **is it for sale?** ¿se vende? [seh vendeh]
salida exit
salidas departures
salmon salmón [sal-mon]
salt sal
same mismo [meez-moh]
  the same again, please lo mismo otra vez, por
  favor [. . . veth . . .]
  the same to you igualmente [eeg-wal-
  menteh]
  it's all the same to me me es igual [meh ess
  eeg-wal]
sand arena [areh-na]
sandal una sandalia [–al-ya]
sandwich sandwich
» TRAVEL TIP: a 'sandwich' will be toasted;
  otherwise ask for 'un bocadillo' [–deeyoh]
sanitary towel una compresa
satisfactory satisfactorio [–tor-yoh]
Saturday sábado
sauce salsa
  saucepan un cazo [kah-thoh]
saucer un platillo [–eeyoh]
sauna una sauna [sah-oo-na]
sausage una salchicha [–chee–]
save (life) salvar
say: **how do you say . . . in Spanish?** ¿cómo se
  dice . . . en español? [. . . seh dee-theh . . .]
  what did he say? ¿qué ha dicho? [keh ah
  dee-choh]
scarf una bufanda [boo–]
  (head) un pañuelo [pan-yweh-loh]

scenery el paisaje [pye-saheh]
schedule un programa
  on/behind schedule en punto/con retraso
  scheduled flight vuelo regular [vweh-loh regoolar]
school la escuela [ess-kweh-la]
scissors: a pair of scissors unas tijeras [tee-heh-rass]
scooter una moto
Scotland Escocia [eskoth-ya]
Scottish escocés [eskothess]
scrambled eggs huevos revueltos [weh-voss rev-weltoss]
scratch (verb) arañar [aran-yar]
scream un chillido [chee-yeedoh]
screw (noun) un tornillo [torneeyoh]
  screwdriver un destornillador [dess-torneeyador]
se alquila habitación room for rent
  se prohibe la entrada no admission/no entry
  se vende for sale
sea el mar
  by the sea junto al mar [hoontoh . . .]
seafood mariscos [–ree–]
search (verb) buscar [boo–]
  search party una expedición de búsqueda [oona esspedeeth-yon deh booss-keh-da]
seasick: I feel seasick estoy mareado [. . . marreh-ah-doh]
  I get seasick me mareo [meh marreh-oh]
seaside la orilla del mar [oreeya . . .]
  let's go to the seaside vámonos a la playa [. . . pla-ya]
season la temporada
  in the high/low season en la temporada alta/baja [. . . bahah]
seasoning condimento
seat el asiento [assee-entoh]
  is this somebody's seat? ¿es de alguien este asiento? [ess deh alg-yen . . .]

seat belt cinturón de seguridad [theentooron deh segooreed*a*]

sea urchin un erizo de mar [err*ee*-thoh deh mar]

seaweed algas

second *(adjective)* segundo [–goo–]
(time) un segundo
just a second! ¡un momento!
second-hand de segunda mano
the second of ... el dos de ...

see ver [vair]
oh, I see ah, ya comprendo
have you seen ...? ¿ha visto usted ...? [ah v*ee*stoh oost*e*h]
can I see the room? ¿puedo ver la habitación? [pw*e*h-doh vair la abbee-tath-y*o*n]

seem parecer [par*e*h-th*air*]
it seems so eso parece [*e*h-soh par*e*h-theh]

seldom rara vez [... veth]

self: self-service autoservicio [*o*w-toh-s*air*- veeth-yoh]

sell vender [vend-*ai*r]

send enviar [embee-*a*r]

sensitive sensible [sens*ee*bleh]

sentimental sentiment*a*l

señoras *ladies*

separate *(adjective)* separado
I'm separated estoy separado
can we pay separately? ¿podemos pag*a*r por separado? [pod*e*h-moss ...]

September septiembre [septee-*e*mbreh]

serious serio [s*e*h-ree-oh]
I'm serious lo digo en serio [... d*e*egoh ...]
this is serious esto es grave [... gr*a*h-veh]
is it serious, doctor? ¿es grave, Doctor?

service: the service was excellent/poor el servicio ha sido excelente/ha dejado bastante que desear [el sair-v*ee*th-yoh ah s*ee*doh esstheh-l*e*nteh/ah deh-*ha*h-doh bass-t*a*nteh keh desseh-*a*r]

....

service station una estación de servicio
[esstath-yon deh sair-veeth-yoh]

servicios *toilets*

serviette una servilleta [sair-veeyeh-ta]

several varios [var-yoss]

sexy sexy

shade: in the shade a la sombra

shake sacudir [sakoodeer]
  to shake hands estrecharse la mano
  [. . . . –seh . . .]

» *TRAVEL TIP: shake hands every time you are
introduced to someone, or when you see someone
after an absence*

shallow poco profundo [. . .–foon-doh]

shame: what a shame! ¡qué lástima! [keh . . .]

shampoo *(noun)* el champú [champoo]

shandy cerveza con limonada [thair-veh-tha kon
leemonah-da]

» *TRAVEL TIP: Spanish beer is usually lager, so it
won't be true shandy*

share *(room, table)* compartir [–teer]

shark un tiburón [teebooron]

sharp afilado
  (taste) ácido [athee-doh]

shave afeitarse [affay-tarseh]
  shaver máquina de afeitar [mackeena deh
affay-tar]
  shaving foam espuma de afeitar
  shaving point enchufe para la máquina de
afeitar [en-choofeh . . .]

she ella [eh-ya]
  does she live here? ¿vive aquí? [vee-veh akee]
  she is my friend es mi amiga [. . . mee . . .]
  she is tired está cansada

sheep una oveja [oveh-ha]

sheet una sábana

shelf un estante [–teh]

shell una concha
  shellfish mariscos [–ree–]

shelter *(noun)* cobijo [kobee-hoh]

....

can we shelter here? ¿podemos cobijarnos aquí? [podeh-moss kobee-*h*arnoss ak*ee*]

herry un jerez [*h*ereth]

hin la espinilla [esspeen*ee*ya]

hip un barco

  by ship en barco

hirt una camisa [kam*ee*-sa]

hock *(noun: surprise)* un susto [s*oo*–]

  what a shock! ¡qué susto! [keh . . .]

  I got an electric shock from the . . . me ha dado un calambre el . . . [meh ah d*a*h-doh . . . kal*a*mbreh . . .]

  shock-absorber un amortiguador [amorteeg-wador]

hoes zapatos [tha–]

> *TRAVEL TIP: shoe sizes*

UK	4	5	6	7	8	9	10	11
Spain	37	38	39	41	42	43	44	46

hop una tienda [tee–]

  I've some shopping to do tengo que hacer unas compras [. . . keh ath-*air* . . .]

hore la orilla [or*ee*ya]

hort corto

  I'm three short me faltan tres [meh . . .]

  short cut un atajo [at*a*h-*h*oh]

horts pantalones cortos [–oness . . .]

houlder el hombro [ombroh]

hout gritar [gree–]

how: please show me por favor, enséñeme [. . . ens*e*n-yeh-meh]

hower: with shower con ducha [d*oo*tcha]

hrimps camarones [–oness]

hrink: it's shrunk se ha encogido [seh ah enkoh-*hee*doh]

hut *(verb)* cerrar [th–]

  when do you shut? ¿cuándo cierran? [kw*a*ndoh thee-*e*rran]

  shut up! ¡a callar! [ah ka-y*a*r]

hy tímido

ick enfermo [–f*air*–]

....

I feel sick estoy mareado [... marreh-*a*h-doh]
he's been sick ha vomitado [ah ...]
side lado
  side lights luces de posición [l*oo*thess deh
  posseeth-y*on*]
  side street una callejuela [ka-yeh-*h*weh-la]
  by the side of the road a un lado de la
  carretera
sight: out of sight fuera de la vista [fweh-
  ra ...]
  the sights of ... los lugares de interés de ...
  [loss loog*a*ress deh eenter*e*ss]
  sightseeing tour un recorrido turístico
  [rekorr*ee*doh too*ree*steekoh]
sign *(roadsign)* una señal [sen-y*a*l]
  (notice) un letrero
signal: he didn't signal no señaló [noh sen-
  yall*oh*]
signature la firma [f*ee*r–]
silence *(noun)* silencio [seelenth-yoh]
silencer el silenciador [seelenth-yad*o*r]
silencio quiet
silk seda [s*e*h-da]
silly tonto
silver plata
similar parecido [parreh-th*ee*doh]
simple sencillo [senth*ee*yoh]
since: since last week desde la semana pasad*a*
  [d*e*z-deh ...]
  since we arrived desde que llegamos [... keh
  yeh-g*a*h-moss]
  (because) como
sincere sincero [seen-th*e*h-roh]
  yours sincerely le saluda atentamente
sing cant*a*r
single: single room una habitación individua*l*
  [abbee-tath-yon eendee-veed-w*a*l]
  I'm single estoy soltero
  a single to ... un billete para ...
  [... beel-yeh-teh ...]

....

sink: it sank se hundió [seh oond-yoh]
sir señor [sen-yor]
sister: my sister mi hermana [mee air-mah-na]
sit: can I sit here? ¿puedo sentarme aquí?
  [pweh-doh sentarmeh akee]
size talla [ta-ya]
ski *(noun)* el esquí [eskee]
  (verb) esquiar [eskee-ar]
  ski boots botas de esquí
  skiing el esquí
  ski-lift telesquí
  ski pants pantalones de esquí [pantaloh-
  ness . . .]
  ski pole un bastón de esquí
  ski slope/run una pista [peesta]
  ski wax cera para esquíes [thera para eskee-
  ess]
skid *(verb)* patinar
skin la piel [pee-ell]
  skin-diving bucear [boo-theh-ar]
skirt una falda
sky el cielo [thee-eh-loh]
  in the sky en el cielo
sleep: I can't sleep no puedo dormir [noh
  pweh-doh dormeer]
sleeper *(rail)* coche-cama [kotcheh–]
sleeping bag saco de dormir [. . . deh dormeer]
sleeping pill una pastilla para dormir [pass-
  teeya . . .]
  YOU MAY HEAR . . .
  ¿ha dormido bien? *did you sleep well?*
sleeve la manga
slide *(phot)* una diapositiva [dee-apossee-teeva]
slow lento
  could you speak a little slower? ¿podría
  hablar un poco más despacio? [podree-a ablar
  oon pokoh mass dess-path-yoh]
small pequeño [peckehn-yoh]
  small change calderilla [kaldereeya]
smallpox viruela [veer-weh-la]

....

smell: there's a funny smell hay un olor raro
[eye . . .]
  it smells huele mal [weh-leh . . .]
smile *(verb)* sonreír [sonn-reh-*eer*]
smoke *(noun)* humo [*oo*moh]
  do you smoke? ¿fuma usted? [*foo*ma oos*teh*]
  can I smoke? ¿puedo fumar? [pweh-doh
foo*mar*]
smooth suave [*swah*-veh]
snack: can we just have a snack? ¿queríamos
tomar sólo una comida ligera [ker*ee*-ah-
moss . . . komm*ee*da lee-*heh*-ra]
snake una serpiente [sair-pee-enteh]
snorkel un respirador
snow nieve [nee-*eh*-veh]
so: it's so hot hace tanto calor [*ah*-theh . . .]
  not so much no tanto
  so-so así, así [ass*ee* . . .]
soap jabón [*h*abon]
  soap powder jabón en polvo
sober sobrio [soh-bree-oh]
sock un calcetín [kal-theh-*teen*]
soda (water) agua de seltz [*ah*-gwa deh selts]
soft drink una bebida no alcohólica [beb*ee*da noh
alko-*o*lleeka]
sole *(shoe)* suela [sweh-la]
  could you put new soles on these? ¿puede
ponerles medias suelas? [pweh-deh pon*air*-less
med-yass sweh-lass]
  YOU MAY THEN HEAR . . .
  ¿de goma o de material? *rubber or leather?*
some: some people algunas personas
[alg*oo*nass pair-s*o*nass]
  can I have some grapes/bread? ¿me pone
unas uvas/un poco de pan? [meh poh-neh *oo*nas
*oo*vass . . .]
  can I have some more? ¿me pone un poco
más? [meh po-neh . . .]
  that's some drink! ¡eso es lo que se dice una
bebida! [. . . keh seh d*ee*theh *oo*na beb*ee*da]

somebody alguien [*a*lg-yen]
something algo
sometime alguna vez [alg*oo*na veth]
sometimes algunas veces [alg*oo*nass veh-thess]
somewhere en algún sitio [alg*oo*n seet-yoh]
son: my son mi hijo [mee *ee-h*oh]
song una canción [kanth-yon]
soon pronto; **sooner** antes [*a*ntess]
  as soon as possible lo antes posible
  [. . . poss*ee*bleh]
sore: it's sore me duele [meh dweh-leh]
  sore throat dolor de garganta
sorry: (I'm) sorry ¡perdón! [pair-d*o*n]
sort: this sort este tipo [*e*ssteh t*ee*poh]
  what sort of . . . ? ¿qué tipo de . . . ? [keh t*ee*poh
  deh . . .]
  will you sort it out? ¿lo puede arreglar? [loh
  pweh-deh . . .]
sótano *basement*
soup sopa
sour agrio [*a*h-gree-oh]
south sur [soor]
South Africa Sudáfrica [sood–]
South African sudafricano
souvenir un recuerdo [rekw*a*ir-doh]
spade una pala
spaghetti espaguetis [–gh*e*tteess]
Spain España [esp*a*n-ya]
Spaniard un español [espan-y*o*l]
Spanish español
  a Spanish woman una española [espan-
  yoh-la]
  the Spanish los españoles [espan-yoh-less]
  I don't speak Spanish no hablo español [noh
  *a*h-bloh . . .]
spanner una llave inglesa [y*a*h-veh eengleh-sa]
spare: spare part una pieza de repuesto [pee-
  *e*h-tha deh repw*e*sstoh]
  spare wheel rueda de recambio [rweh-da deh
  rek*a*mb-yoh]

....

spark(ing) plug una bujía [boo-*hee*-a]
speak: do you speak English? ¿habla inglés?
[*a*h-bla eengl*ess*]
   I don't speak ... no hablo ... [noh *a*h-bloh]
special especial [esspeth-y*a*l]
specialist especialista [esspeth-yal*ee*sta]
specially especialmente [–teh]
spectacles unas gafas
speed velocidad [velothee-d*a*]
   he was speeding iba con exceso de velocidad
[*ee*ba kon ess-th*ess*oh ...]
   speed limit límite de velocidad
[*lee*meeteh ...]
   speedometer el cuentakilómetros [kwenta-
kee-l*o*mmetross]
spend *(money)* gastar
spice una especia [essp*e*th-ya]
   is it spicy? ¿es picante? [... peek*a*nteh]
   it's too spicy es demasiado picante [...
demass-y*a*h-doh ...]
spider una araña [ar*a*hn-ya]
spirits licores [leek*o*ress]
spoon una cuchara [koo–]
sprain: I've sprained my ... me he torcido
el ... [meh eh torth*ee*doh ...]
spring *(water)* un manantial [–y*a*l]
   (season) la primavera [preema-v*eh*-ra]
   (of car, seat etc) un muelle [mweh-yeh]
square *(in town)* una plaza [–tha]
   two square metres dos metros cuadrados
[... kwadr*a*h-doss]
stairs la escalera
stale duro [d*oo*roh]
stall: it keeps stalling no hace más que calarse
[noh *a*h-theh mass keh kal*a*r-seh]
stalls butacas de patio [boot*a*h-kass deh pat-yoh]
stamp un sello [seh-yoh]
   two stamps for England dos sellos para
Inglaterra
» *TRAVEL TIP: stamps are usually bought at*

*'estancos' (tobacco shops); look for red and
yellow stripes around entrance*
stand *(verb)* estar de pie [. . . pee-*eh*]
  (noun: at fair) un stand
standard *(adjective)* normal
star una estrella [esstreh-ya]
starboard estribor
start el comienzo [kom-yenthoh]
  my car won't start mi coche no arranca [mee
  kotcheh noh . . .]
  when does it start? ¿cuándo empieza?
  [kwandoh emp-yetha]
starter *(car)* el motor de arranque [. . . deh
  arrankeh]
starving: I'm starving estoy muerto de hambre
  [. . . mwairtoh deh ambreh]
station la estación [esstath-yon]
statue una estatua [esstat-wa]
stay: we enjoyed our stay hemos disfrutado
  mucho de nuestra estancia [eh-moss
  deesfrootah-doh mootchoh deh nwesstra
  estanth-ya]
  stay there quédese ahí [keh-deh-seh ah-ee]
  I'm staying at . . . estoy en . . .
steak un filete [feeleh-teh]
  YOU MAY HEAR . . .
  ¿muy hecho? [mwee etchoh] *well done?*
  ¿poco hecho? *rare?*
  if you like it medium ask for 'normal'
steep empinado
steering *(car)* la dirección [deerekth-yon]
  steering wheel el volante [–teh]
step *(noun: of stair)* un escalón
stereo estéreo [essteh-reh-oh]
sterling libras esterlinas [leebrass esstair-
  leenass]
stewardess la azafata [atha–]
sticking plaster una tirita [teereeta]
sticky pegajoso [–hosoh]
stiff *(door etc)* duro [doo-roh]

still *(adjective)* **keep still** estése quieto [essteh-seh kee-eh-toh]
  I'm still here todavía estoy aquí [toda-vee-a esstoy akee]

stink *(noun)* mal olor

stolen: my wallet's been stolen me han robado la cartera [meh an . . .]

stomach el estómago
  I've got stomach-ache me duele el vientre [meh dweh-leh el vee-entreh]
  have you got something for an upset stomach? ¿tiene algo para el dolor de estómago? [tee-eh-neh . . .]

stone una piedra [pee-eh-dra]
» *TRAVEL TIP: 1 stone = 6.35 kilos*

stop: stop! ¡deténgase! [deh-tenga-seh]
  stop-over una escala
  do you stop near . . .? ¿para usted cerca de . . .? [pah-ra oosteh thairka deh]

storm una tormenta

straight derecho
  go straight on siga derecho [seega . . .]
  straight away en seguida [en seh-gheeda]
  straight whisky un whisky solo

strange *(odd)* extraño [esstran-yoh]
  (unknown) desconocido [–theedoh]

stranger un desconocido
  I'm a stranger here soy forastero aquí [. . . akee]

strap correa [korreh-a]

strawberry una fresa [freh-sa]

street una calle [ka-yeh]

string: have you got any string? ¿tiene usted cuerda? [tee-eh-neh oosteh kwairda]

striptease estriptis [esstreepteess]

stroke: he's had a stroke ha sufrido un infarto [ah soofreedoh . . .]

strong fuerte [fwairteh]

student estudiante [esstood-yanteh]

stung: I've been stung (by a jellyfish) me ha

picado (una medusa) [meh ah peek*a*h-doh oona med*oo*sa]

tupid estúpido [–*too*–]

uch: such a lot tanto

uddenly de repente [deh reh-p*e*nteh]

ugar azúcar [ath*oo*–]

uit un traje [tr*a*h-*h*eh]

   suitcase una maleta [–l*e*h–]

uitable adecuado [adekw*a*h-doh]

ummer verano [ver*a*h-noh]

un el sol

   in the sun al sol

   out of the sun a la sombra

   sunbathe tomar el sol

   sunburn una quemadura sol*a*r [keh-mad*oo*ra . . .]

   sunglasses unas gafas de sol

   suntan un bronceado [bronth*e*h-*a*h-doh]

   sunstroke una insolación [–ath-yon]

   suntan oil un bronceador [bronth*e*h-ad*o*r]

unday domingo

upermarket un supermerc*a*do [–mair–]

upper la cena [th*e*h-na]

ure: I'm not sure no estoy seguro

   sure! ¡claro que sí! [. . . keh see]

   are you sure? ¿est*á* usted seguro? [o*o*steh seg*oo*roh]

urfboard plancha de hacer surf [. . . ath-*ai*r soorf]; **to go surfing** ir a hacer surf [eer ah ath*ai*r . . .]

urname apellido [appeh-y*ee*doh]

wear word un taco

weat *(verb)* sudar [soo–]

weet: it's too sweet es demasiado dulce [demass-y*a*h-doh d*oo*ltheh]

   (dessert) postre [poss-treh]

   sweets caramelos [–m*e*h–]

werve: I had to swerve tuve que torcer bruscamente [t*oo*veh keh torth-*ai*r brooskam*e*nteh]

swim: I'm going for a swim me voy a dar un baño [... ban-yoh]

swimming costume el traje de baño [trah-hel deh ban-yoh]

let's go for a swim vamos a bañarnos [bah-moss ah ban-yarnoss]

swimming pool una piscina [peess-theena]

switch *(noun)* el interruptor [–roop–]

to switch on/off encender/apagar [enthend-air ...]

table una mesa [meh-sa]

a table for 4 una mesa para cuatro persona [... kwatroh pair– ...]

table wine vino de mesa

take coger [kohair]

can I take this with me? ¿puedo llevarme esto? [pweh-doh yeh-var-meh ...]

will you take me to the airport? ¿quiere llevarme al aeropuerto? [kee-eh-reh ... ah-airo-pwairtoh]

how long will it take? ¿cuánto tiempo tardará? [kwantoh tee-empoh ...]

somebody has taken my bags se han llevad mis maletas [seh an yeh-vah-doh meess ...]

can I take you out tonight? ¿quieres salir conmigo esta noche? [kee-eh-ress saleer konmeegoh essta notchee]

is this seat taken? ¿está ocupado este asiento [... ass-yentoh]

talcum powder polvos de talco

talk *(verb)* hablar [ablar]

tall alto

tampons tampones [–oness]

tan un bronceado [brontheh-ah-doh]

I want to get a tan quiero broncearmc [kee-eh-roh brontheh-armeh]

tank *(of car)* el depósito [deh-possee-toh]

tap el grifo [greefoh]

tape una cinta [theenta]

tape recorder un magnetofón

taquilla *ticket office*

tariff la tarifa [−ree−]

taste *(noun)* sabor
  can I taste it? ¿puedo probarlo? [pweh-doh . . .]
  it tastes horrible/very nice sabe a rayos/muy
  bien [sah-beh ah ra-yoss/mwee bee-en]

taxi un taxi
  will you get me a taxi? ¿quiere buscarme un
  taxi? [kee-eh-reh booskarmeh . . .]
  where can I get a taxi? ¿dónde puedo coger un
  taxi? [dondeh pweh-doh kohair . . .]
  taxi-driver el taxista [−eesta]

tea té [teh]
  could I have a cup of tea? ¿me pone un té, por
  favor? [meh poneh . . .]
» *TRAVEL TIP: unless you ask otherwise, tea is
  normally served without milk; if you want it
  with milk say 'con leche'* [kon leh-cheh]
  YOU MAY HEAR . . .
  '¿con limón?' *with lemon?*

teach: could you teach me? ¿podría
  enseñarme? [podree-a ensen-yarmeh]
  could you teach me Spanish? ¿podría
  enseñarme español? [. . . ess-pan-yol]

teacher el profesor

telegram un telegrama
  I want to send a telegram quiero mandar un
  telegrama [kee-eh-roh . . .]

telephone *(noun)* el teléfono [telleffonoh]
  can I make a phone-call? ¿puedo hacer una
  llamada telefónica? [pweh-doh ath-air oona
  yamah-da . . .]
  can I speak to . . .? ¿se puede poner . . .? [seh
  pweh-deh ponair]
  could you get the number for me? *(dial)*
  ¿podría marcarme usted el número? [podree-a
  markar-meh oosteh el noomeh-roh]
  telephone directory la guía telefónica
  [ghee-a tellefonneeka]
» *TRAVEL TIP: money in first, then dial; unused*

....

coins will be returned; code for UK is 07, wait for
high-pitched tone, then 44 followed by number;
omit first 0 of UK area code

television la televisión [–vees-yon]

I'd like to watch television quisiera ver la
televisión [kees-yeh-ra vair la tellevees-yon]

tell: could you tell me where . . .? ¿podría
decirme dónde . . .? [podree-a detheer-meh
dondeh]

temperature (weather etc) la temperatura
[–toora]

he's got a temperature tiene fiebre [tee-
eh-neh fee-eh-breh]

tennis el tenis [teh-neess]

tennis court una pista de tenis [peesta . . .]

tennis racquet una raqueta de tenis
[rackeh-ta . . .]

tennis ball una pelota de tenis

tent una tienda de campaña [tee-enda deh
kampan-ya]

terminus la estación terminal [estath-yon
tairmeenal]

terrible terrible [terreebleh]

terrific fabuloso [–boo–]

than que [keh]

bigger than más grande que [. . . –deh . . .]

fewer than 5 menos de cinco [meh-noss deh
theenkoh]

thanks, thank you gracias [grath-yass]

no thank you no gracias

thank you very much muchas gracias

thank you for your help gracias por su ayuda

YOU MAY THEN HEAR . . .

de nada you're welcome

that: that man/that table ese hombre/esa mesa
[eh-seh ombreh/eh-sa meh-sa]

I would like that one quiero ese [kee-eh-roh
eh-seh]

how do you say that? ¿cómo se dice eso? [. . .
seh deetheh eh-soh]

I think that ... creo que ... [kreh-oh keh]
the *(singular)* el; la *(plural)* los; las
theatre el teatro [teh-ah-troh]
their su; sus [soo; sooss]
  it's their bag, it's theirs es su bolso, es (el) suyo [... sooyo]
them *(objects)* los; las
  (persons) les [less]
  with/for them con/para ellos [... eh-yoss]
  who? – them ¿quiénes? – ellos
then entonces [enton-thess]
there allí [a-yee]
  how do I get there? ¿cómo se llega? [... seh yeh-ga]
  is there .../are there ...? ¿hay ...? [eye]
  there you are *(giving something)* tome [toh-meh]
these estos; estas
  can I take these? ¿puedo coger éstos? [pweh-doh kohair esstoss]
they ellos; ellas [eh-yoss/eh-yass]
  they are son, están
thick grueso [grweh-soh]
  (stupid) estúpido [–too–]
thief un ladrón
thigh el muslo [moozloh]
thin delgado
thing una cosa
  I've lost all my things he perdido todas mis cosas [eh pairdeedoh ...]
think pensar
  I'll think it over lo pensaré [... pensareh]
  I think so/I don't think so creo que sí/no creo [kreh-oh keh see ...]
third *(adjective)* tercero [tair-theh-roh]
thirsty: I'm thirsty tengo sed [... seth]
this este; esta
  this hotel/this street este hotel/esta calle [essteh o-tel/esta ka-yeh]
  can I have this one? ¿me da éste?

this is my wife/this is Mr ... ésta es mi mujer/éste es el señor ... [... mee moo-*hair* ...]
  is this ...? ¿es esto ...?
those esos; esas
  how much are those? ¿cuánto valen esos? [kwantoh vah-len *eh*-soss]
thread *(noun)* hilo [*eeloh*]
throat la garganta
throttle *(motorbike, boat)* el acelerador [atheh-leh-rad*or*]
through a través de [ah travess deh]
throw *(verb)* tirar [tee–]
thumb el dedo pulgar [d*eh*-doh poolg*ar*]
thunder *(noun)* un trueno [trw*eh*-noh]
  thunderstorm una tormenta
Thursday jueves [*h*weh-vess]
ticket *(train, bus, plane, boat)* un billete [beey*eh*-teh]
  (cinema) una entrada
  (cloakroom) un ticket [tee-keh]
tie *(necktie)* una corbata
tight *(clothes)* ajustado [ah*oos*–]
  they're too tight son demasiado ajustados [demass-yah-doh ah*oos*stah-doss]
tights unos leotardos [*oo*noss leh-o-tardoss]
time el tiempo [tee-*empoh*]
  what's the time? ¿qué hora es? [keh *ora* ess]
  I haven't got time no tengo tiempo
  for the time being por el momento
  this time/last time/next time esta vez/la última vez/la próxima vez [... veth]
  three times tres veces [tress v*eth*ess]
  have a good time! ¡que se divierta! [keh seh deev-y*air*ta]
  timetable el horario [or-*ar*-yoh]
» *TRAVEL TIP: how to tell the time*
  it's one o'clock es la una [*oona*]
  it's two/three/four o'clock son las dos/tres/cuatro [doss/tress/kw*a*troh]

it's 5/10/20/25 past seven son las siete y cinco/diez/veinte/veinticinco [ee theenkoh/dee-eth/vainteh/vaintee-theenkoh]

it's quarter past eight/eight fifteen son las ocho y cuarto [ee kwartoh]

it's half past nine/nine thirty son las nueve y media [nweh-veh ee maid-ya]

it's 25/20/10/5 to ten son las diez menos veinticinco/veinte/diez/cinco [meh-noss]

it's quarter to eleven/10.45 son las once menos cuarto [ontheh meh-noss kwartoh]

it's twelve o'clock (am/pm) son las doce (de la mañana/de la noche) [doh-theh deh la man-yah-na/deh la notcheh]

at one o'clock a la una [ah . . .]

at three thirty a las tres y media [ah lass tress ee maid-ya]

tin (can) una lata

   tin-opener un abrelatas [ah-breh-lah-tass]

tip (noun) una propina [–pee–]

   is the tip included? ¿va incluída la propina? [. . . eenklweeda . . .]

» TRAVEL TIP: 10% is usual; tip same people as in UK; but usherettes will also expect a tip

tired cansado

   I'm tired estoy cansado

tissues kleenex

to: to Madrid/England a Madrid/Inglaterra [ah madree . . .]

toast una tostada

   (drinking) un brindis [breendeess]

tobacco tabaco

tobacconist's el estanco

today hoy [oy]

toe un dedo del pie [deh-doh del pee-eh]

together junto [hoontoh]

   we're together venimos juntos [veneemoss . . .]

   can we pay all together? ¿puede cobrarlo todo junto? [pweh-deh . . .]

toilet los aseos [ass-*eh*-oss]
  where are the toilets? ¿dónde están los aseos?
  I have to go to the toilet tengo que ir al wáter
  [. . . keh eer al v*a*ttair]
  there's no toilet paper no hay papel higiénico
  [no eye pap*e*l ee*h*-yeh-neekoh]
» *TRAVEL TIP: not many public conveniences;*
  usually in stations; don't hesitate to go into a bar
  or café and use their toilet; that's normal
tomato tomate [toh-m*a*h-teh]
  tomato ketchup catsup (de tomate) [kat-
  *soo*p . . .]
  tomato juice zumo de tomate [th*oo*-moh . . .]
tomorrow mañana [man-y*a*h-na]
  tomorrow morning/tomorrow afternoon/
  tomorrow evening mañana por la mañana/
  mañana por la tarde/mañana por la noche
  [. . . t*a*rdeh/. . . n*o*tcheh]
  the day after tomorrow pasado mañana
  see you tomorrow hasta mañana [*a*sta . . .]
ton una tonelada [tonneh-l*a*h-da]
» *TRAVEL TIP: 1 ton = 1,016 kilos*
tongue la lengua [l*e*ng-gwa]
tonic (water) tónica
tonight esta noche [. . . n*o*tcheh]
tonne una tonelada métrica
» *TRAVEL TIP: 1 tonne = 1000 kilos = metric ton*
tonsils las amígdalas [am*ee*gdalass]
tonsillitis amigdalitis [–*ee*teess]
too demasiado [demass-y*a*h-doh] *(also)* también
  [tamb-yen]
  that's too much eso es demasiado
tool una herramienta [erram-yenta]
tooth un diente [dee-*e*nteh]
  (back teeth) las muelas [mw*e*h-lass]
  I've got toothache tengo dolor de muelas
  toothbrush un cepillo de dientes [thep*ee*yoh]
  toothpaste pasta dentífrica [. . . dent*ee*freeka]
top: on top of . . . encima de [enth*ee*ma deh]
  on the top floor en el ú*l*timo piso [. . . p*ee*-soh]

at the top en lo alto
torch una linterna [leentairna]
total *(noun)* el total
tough *(meat)* dura [doora]
tour *(noun)* un viaje [vee-ah-heh]
  we'd like to go on a tour of . . . nos gustaría
  hacer un viaje por . . . [noss goostaree-a ath-
  air . . .]
  we're touring around estamos de turismo
  [. . . tooreezmoh]
tourist turista [tooreess-ta]
  I'm a tourist soy un turista
  tourist office la oficina de turismo
  [offeetheena deh tooreezmoh]
tow *(verb)* remolcar
  can you give me a tow? ¿puede usted
  remolcarme? [pweh-deh oosteh . . .]
  towrope un cable de remolque [kah-bleh deh
  remol-keh]
towards hacia [ath-ya]
  he was coming straight towards me venía
  derecho hacia mí [venee-a derecho ath-ya mee]
towel una toalla [toh-ah-ya]
town una ciudad [thee-ooda]
  (smaller) un pueblo [pweh-bloh]
  in town en el centro [. . . thentroh]
  would you take me into the town? ¿podría
  llevarme al centro? [podree-a yeh-var-meh . . .]
traditional tradicional [tradeeth-yonal]
  a traditional Spanish meal una comida
  española tradicional [. . . kommeeda . . .]
traffic el tráfico
  traffic lights los semáforos
  traffic policeman un guardia de la
  circulación [gwar-dee-a deh la theer-koo-
  lath-yon]
train el tren
  » *TRAVEL TIP: important to book in advance as*
  trains tend to be crowded; train travel is slow
tranquillizers calmantes [–tess]

....

translate traducir [−oot*h*eer]
   would you translate that for me? ¿quiere usted traducirme eso, por favor? [kee-*e*h-reh oost*e*h tradoot*h*eer-meh . . .]
transmission *(of car)* la transmisión [transmeess-yon]
travel agent's una agencia de viajes [a*h*enth-ya deh vee-a*h*-*h*ess]
   traveller's cheque un cheque de viaje [ch*e*h-keh deh vee-a*h*-*h*eh]
tree un *á*rbol
tremendous tremendo
trim: just a trim please recórtemelo nada más, por favor [reh-k*o*rteh-meh-loh . . .]
trip *(noun)* una excursión [ess-koors-yon]
   we want to go on a trip to . . . queremos hacer una excursión a . . . [kereh-moss ath-*air* . . .]
trouble *(noun)* problemas
   I'm having trouble with . . . estoy teniendo problemas con . . . [. . . ten-yendoh problehmass . . .]
trousers unos pantalones [−loh-ness]
true verdadero [vair-dad*e*h-roh]
   it's not true no es verdad [. . . vair-d*a*]
trunks *(swimming)* un bañador (de hombre) [ban-ya-d*o*r deh *o*mbreh]
try *(verb)* intent*a*r
   please try haga el favor de intentarlo [a*h*-ga . . .]
   can I try it on? ¿puedo probármelo? [pweh-doh proh-b*a*r-meh-loh]
T-shirt una camiseta [kamee-s*e*h-ta]
Tuesday martes [−tess]
tunnel un túnel [t*oo*nell]
turn: where do we turn off? ¿dónde tenemos que desviarnos? [d*o*ndeh ten-*e*h-moss keh dess-vee-*a*rnoss]
   he turned without indicating giró sin señalar [*h*ee-roh seen sen-yal*a*r]

twice dos veces [. . . vethess]
  twice as much dos veces más
twin beds dos camas
two dos [doss]
typewriter una máquina de escribir [mackeena deh esskreebeer]
typical típico [tee–]
tyre una rueda [rweh-da]
  I need a new tyre necesito una rueda nueva [nethesseetoh oona rweh-da nweh-va]
» *TRAVEL TIP: tyre pressures*

lb/sq in	18	20	22	24	26	28	30
kg/sq cm	1.3	1.4	1.5	1.7	1.8	2	2.1

ugly feo [feh-oh]
ulcer una úlcera [ool-theh-ra]
Ulster Ulster [oolstair]
umbrella un paraguas [parahg-wass]
uncle: my uncle mi tío [mee tee-oh]
uncomfortable incómodo
unconscious inconsciente [–sthee-enteh]
under debajo de [debah-hoh deh]
underdone poco hecho [. . . etchoh]
underground *(rail)* el metro
understand: I understand lo comprendo
  I don't understand no entiendo [noh ent-yendoh]
  do you understand? ¿entiende usted? [ent-yendeh oosteh]
undo deshacer [dess-ath-air]
unfriendly antipático [antee-pattekoh]
unhappy desgraciado [dess-grath-yah-doh]
United States Estados Unidos [esstah-doss ooneedoss]
unlock abrir [abreer]
untie desatar
until hasta que [asta keh]
  until next year hasta el año que viene [asta el an-yoh keh vee-eh-neh]
unusual poco corriente [. . . korr-yenteh]
up arriba [arreeba]

....

he's not up yet todavía no se ha levantado [toh-dav*ee*-a noh seh ah . . .]
  what's up? ¿qué pasa? [keh . . .]
upside down al revés [al reh-v*ess*]
upstairs arriba [arr*ee*ba]
urgent urgente [oor-*h*enteh]
us nos [noss]
  with/for us con/para nosotros [. . . noss*oh*-tross]
  who? – us ¿quiénes? – nosotros
use: can I use . . .? ¿puedo usar . . .? [pweh-doh oos*ar*]
useful útil [*oo*teel]
usual habitual [abbeet-w*al*]
  as usual como de costumbre [. . . deh koss-t*oo*m-breh]
usually normalmente [–teh]
U-turn un viraje en U [veer*a*h-*h*eh en oo]
vacancy: do you have any vacancies? *(hotel)* ¿tiene alguna habitación libre? [tee-*eh*-neh algoona abbee-tath-yon l*ee*breh]
vacate *(room)* desocupar [–koo–]
vaccination una vacuna [–koo–]
vacuum flask un termo [t*air*-moh]
valid válido
  how long is it valid for? ¿hasta cuándo tiene validez? [*a*sta kw*a*ndoh tee-*e*h-neh valeed*e*th]
valley un valle [v*a*-yeh]
valuable valioso [val-y*o*soh]
  will you look after my valuables? ¿quiere cuidar de mis objetos de valor? [kee-*e*h-reh kweed*a*r deh meess ob-*h*eh-toss deh valor]
value *(noun)* valor
valve una válvula [–voo–]
van una furgoneta [foor-gonn*e*h-ta]
vanilla vainilla [vye-n*ee*yah]
varicose veins varices [var*ee*thess]
Vd., Vds. = **usted, ustedes** *you*
veal ternera [tair-n*e*h-rah]
vegetables verduras [vair-d*oo*rass]

vegetarian *(noun)* vegetariano [ve*h*etarree-*a*h-noh]
velocidad limitada *speed limit*
venta de sellos *stamps*
ventilator el ventilado*r*
very muy [mwee]
    very much mucho [moo–]
via por
village un pueblo [pweh-bloh]
vine una vid [v*ee*the]
vinegar vinagre [veen*a*h-greh]
vineyard un viñedo [veen-ye*h*-doh]
vintage cosecha
    vintage wine vino añejo [ve*e*no an-yeh-*h*oh]
violent violento [vee-o-lentoh]
visibility visibilidad [veeseebeeleed*a*]
visit *(verb)* visitar [veeseet*a*r]
vodka vodka
voice una voz [voth]
voltage voltaje [voll-t*a*h-*h*eh]
waist la cintura [theent*oo*ra]
» *TRAVEL TIP: waist measurements*

UK	24	26	28	30	32	34	36	38
Spain	61	66	71	76	80	87	91	97

wait: will we have to wait long? ¿tendremos
    que esperar mucho? [tendr*e*h-moss keh esspeh-
    r*a*r m*oo*choh]
    wait for me espéreme [essp*e*h-reh-meh]
    I'm waiting for a friend/my wife estoy
    esperando a un amigo/a mi mujer [. . . mee
    moo-*h*air]
waiter un camarero [–reh-roh]
    waiter! ¡camarero!
» *TRAVEL TIP: it's not rude to click your fingers to
    get the waiter*
waitress una camarera
    waitress! ¡señorita! [sen-yore*e*ta]
wake: will you wake me up at 7.30? ¿quiere
    despertarme a las siete y media? [kee-*e*h-reh
    dess-pair-t*a*rmeh ah lass see-*e*h-teh ee m*a*id-ya]

....

Wales Gales [gah-less]
walk: can we walk there? ¿se puede ir a pie?
[seh pweh-deh eer ah pee-eh]
  are there any good walks around here?
¿hay algún sitio bonito por donde pasear acqui?
[algoon seet-yoh bonneetoh por dondeh
passeh-ar akee]
  walking shoes zapatos de campo [thapah-
toss . . .]
  walking stick un bastón
wall una pared [parreh]
wallet la cartera [karteh-ra]
want: I want a . . . quiero un/una . . . [kee-eh-
roh . . .]
  I want to talk to . . . quiero hablar
con . . . [kee-eh-roh ablar . . .]
  what do you want? ¿qué quiere usted? [keh
kee-eh-reh oosteh]
  I don't want to no quiero (hacerlo) [noh kee-
eh-roh ath-air-loh]
  he wants to . . . quiere . . .
warm: it's warm today hoy hace calor [oy ah-
theh . . .]
  I feel very warm tengo mucho calor
warning aviso [aveesoh]
was: I was/he was (yo) era; estaba/(él) era;
estaba
  it was era; estaba [eh-ra . . .]
wash: can you wash these for me? ¿podría
lavármelos? [podree-a lavar-meh-loss]
  where can I wash . . .? ¿dónde puedo
lavar . . .? [dondeh pweh-doh . . .]
  washing machine una lavadora
  washing powder jabón en polvo [habon . . .]
washer *(for bolt etc)* una arandela
wasp una avispa [–vee–]
watch *(wrist-)* el reloj [reh-loh]
  will you watch my bags for me? ¿me podría
vigilar las maletas? [meh podree-a veeheelar]
  watch out! ¡cuidado! [kweedah-doh]

water agua [*a*hg-wa]
  can I have some water? ¿puede traerme
  agua? [pweh-deh trah-*ai*rmeh *a*hg-wa]
  hot and cold running water agua caliente y
  fría [. . . kal-yenteh ee fr*ee*-a]
  waterproof impermeable [eempair-meh-
  *a*h-bleh]
  waterskiing esquí acuático [essk*ee*
  akw*a*tteekoh]

way: we'd like to eat the Spanish way
  quisiéramos comer a la española [keess-yeh-
  ramoss kom*ai*r ah la esspan-yola]
  could you tell me the way to . . .? ¿podría
  indicarme el camino para . . .? [podr*ee*-a . . .]
  see **where** *for answers*

we nosotros [noss*o*h-tross]
  we are English somos ingleses [. . . eengleh-
  sess]
  we are tired estamos cansados

weak *(person)* débil [d*e*h-beel]

weather el tiempo [tee-*e*mpoh]
  what filthy weather! ¡qué tiempo tan
  asqueroso! [keh tee-*e*mpoh tan asskeh-r*o*soh]
  what's the weather forecast? ¿cuál es el
  pronóstico del tiempo? [kwal ess . . .]
  YOU MAY THEN HEAR . . .
  va a hacer sol [vah ath-*ai*r sol] *it'll be sunny*
  va a llover [. . . yoh-v*ai*r] *it's going to rain*
  va a mejorar el tiempo [. . . meh-*h*orar el
  tee-*e*mpoh] *it'll improve*

Wednesday miércoles [mee-*ai*r-koless]

week una semana
  a week today/tomorrow de hoy/de mañana
  en una semana [deh oy . . .]
  at the weekend el fin de semana
  [el feen . . .]

weight peso [p*e*h-soh]

well: I'm not feeling well no me encuentro bien
  [noh meh enkw*e*ntroh bee-*e*n]
  he's not well no está bueno [. . . bw*e*h-noh]

....

how are you? very well, thanks ¿cómo está
usted? muy bien, graciae [. . . oost*e*h? mwee
bee-*e*n gr*a*th-yass]

you speak English very well usted habla
inglés muy bien [oost*e*h *a*h-bla eengl*e*ss mwe*e*
bee-*e*n]

wellingtons una botas de agua [. . . deh *a*hg-
wa]

were: **you were** *(singular)* (tú) eras/estabas;
(usted) era/estaba

you were *(plural)* (vosotros) *é*rais/est*á*bais
[eh-ra-eess/esstah-bah-ee*s*s]; (ustedes)
eran/estaban

see **you**

we were (nosotros) *é*ramos/est*á*bamos

they were (ellos) eran/estaban

Welsh galés [gal*e*ss]

west oeste [o-*e*steh]

West Indian antillano [anteey*a*h-noh]

West Indies las Antillas [ant*ee*yass]

wet mojado [m*o*h*a*h-doh]

wet suit un traje isotérmico [trah-*h*eh eesso-
t*a*ir-meekoh]

what que [keh]

what is that? ¿qué es eso? [keh ess *e*h-soh]

what for? ¿para qué?

what's that in Spanish? ¿cómo se llama eso
en español? [. . . seh y*a*ma . . .]

wheel la rueda [roo-*e*h-da]

when cuando [kw*a*ndoh]

when is breakfast? ¿a qué hora es el
desayuno? [ah keh *o*ra . . .]

where donde [d*o*ndeh]

where is the post office? ¿dónde está la
oficina de Correos? [. . . offeeth*e*ena deh
korr*e*h-oss]

YOU MAY THEN HEAR . . .

siga derecho [s*e*ega deh-retchoh] *carry straigh*
on

la primera/segunda a la izquierda/derecha

....

[... eeth-kee-*airda* ...] *first/second on the left/right*

hich que [keh]
  which one? ¿cuál? [kwal]
YOU MAY THEN HEAR...
  éste/ésta *this one*
  ése/ésa *that one*
  aquel/aquella [ak*e*ll/ak*e*h-ya] *that one there*
hisky whisky
hite blanco
hitsun Pentecost*é*s
ho quien [kee-*e*n]
hose cuyo [k*oo*-yoh]
  whose is this? ¿de quién es esto? [deh kee-
  *e*n ...]
YOU MAY THEN HEAR...
  es mío/es mía [m*ee*-oh/m*ee*-a] *it's mine*
hy por qué [... keh]
  why not? ¿por qué no?
ide ancho
ife: my wife mi mujer [mee moo-*hair*]
ill: when will it be finished? ¿cuándo estará
  terminado? [kw*a*ndoh esst*a*ra tair-meen*a*h-
  doh]
  will you do it? ¿lo puede hacer? [loh pw*e*h-deh
  ath-*air*]
I will come back volveré [vol-veh-*reh*]
in gan*a*r
  who won? ¿quién ha ganado? [kee-*e*n ah ...]
ind *(noun)* el viento [vee-*e*ntoh]
indow la ventana
  (of shop) el escaparate [–*a*h-teh]
  near the window cerca de la ventana
  [th*a*irka ...]
indscreen el parabrisas [parabr*ee*-sass]
  windscreen wipers los limpiaparabrisas
  [l*ee*mp-ya–]
indy: it's too windy hace demasiado viento
  [*a*h-theh demass-y*a*h-doh vee-*e*ntoh]
ine vino

....

can I see the wine list? ¿me enseña la lista d
vinos? [meh ensen-ya la leesta deh vee-noss]

» *TRAVEL TIP:*

blanco/tinto/rosado: *white/red/rosé*
jerez fino/amontillado/oloroso: *dry/medium*
cream sherry
Jumilla: *dry, red wines*
Málaga: *very sweet; try Málaga Virgen*
Penedés: *good Catalan wines, especially*
whites and sparkling; try Torres
Rioja: *arguably the best, especially reds; try*
Marqués de Cáceres, Privilegio, Cerro Añón,
Carta de Oro/Berberana
Váldepeñas: *young, mainly red, wines*
Sangría: *red wine, lemonade, brandy and suga*
mix, with sliced apple and oranges

winter invierno [eembee-air-noh]
wire un alambre [–breh]
  (elec) un cable eléctrico [. . . kah-bleh . . .]
with con
without sin [seen]
witness *(noun)* un testigo [tessteegoh]
  will you act as a witness for me? ¿quiere
  usted actuar como testigo mío? [kee-eh-reh
  oosteh ak-too-ar komoh tessteegoh mee-oh]
woman una mujer [moo-hair]
  women las mujeres [moo-heh-ress]
wonderful estupendo [–too–]
won't: it won't start no arranca
wood madera [madeh-ra]
  (forest) un bosque [bosskeh]
wool lana
word una palabra
  I don't know that word no conozco esa
  palabra [no konothko . . .]
work *(verb)* trabajar [trabahar]
  it's not working no funciona [foonth-yonah]
  I work in London trabajo en Londres
  [trabah-hoh en londress]
worry una preocupación [preh-okkoo-path-yo

I'm worried about him estoy preocupado por él

don't worry no se preocupe [noh seh preh-ok*oo*peh]

worse: it's worse es peor [peh-*or*]

he's getting worse está empeorando

worst el peor [peh-*or*]

worth: it's not worth that much no vale tanto [. . . v*a*h-leh . . .]

is it worthwhile going to . . . ? ¿vale la pena ir a . . . ? [v*a*h-leh la p*e*h-na eer ah]

wrap: could you wrap it up? ¿me lo envuelve? [meh loh embw*e*l-veh]

wrench *(noun: tool)* una llave inglesa [y*a*h-veh eengl*e*h-sa]

wrist la muñeca [moon-y*e*h-ka]

write escribir [esskreeb*ee*r]

could you write it down? ¿puede escribírmelo? [pw*e*h-deh esskreeb*ee*r-meh-loh]

I'll write to you le escribiré [leh esskreebeer*e*h]

writing paper papel de escribir

wrong: I think the bill's wrong me parece que la cuenta está equivocada [meh par*e*h-theh keh la kw*e*nta est*a* eh-keevoh-k*a*h-da]

there's something wrong with . . . le pasa algo a . . . [leh . . . ah . . .]

you're wrong se equivoca [seh eh-keevoh-ka]

sorry, wrong number perdone, me he equivocado de número [pairdoh-neh, meh eh eh-keevo-k*a*h-doh deh n*oo*meh-roh]

X-ray una radiografía [raddee-ograf*ee*-a]

yacht un yate [y*a*h-teh]

yard una yarda

» *TRAVEL TIP: 1 yard = 91.44 cms = 0.91 m*

year un año [*a*n-yoh]

this year/next year este año/el año que viene [. . . keh vee-*e*h-neh]

yellow amarillo [–*ee*yoh]

yes sí [see]

....

yesterday ayer [ah-y*air*]
  the day before yesterday anteayer [anteh-
  ah-y*air*]
  yesterday morning/afternoon ayer por la
  mañana/tarde [. . . man-y*a*h-na/t*a*rdeh]
yet: is it ready yet? ¿está listo ya?
  not yet todavía no [todav*ee*-a]
yoghurt yogur [yog*oo*r]
you tú/usted/vosotros/ustedes [too/oost*e*h/. . ./
  oost*e*h-dess]
  I don't understand you no le entiendo [noh
  leh ent-yen-doh]
  with you contigo [--t*ee*--]; con usted
  » *TRAVEL TIP: use 'usted/ustedes' in most*
  situations; the forms 'tu/vosotros' are only used
  for people you know well
young joven [*h*oh-ven]
your tu/su/vuestro [too/soo/vw*e*sstroh]
  is this your camera? ¿es suya esta máquina?
  [ess *s*ooya *e*sta m*a*ckeena]
  is this yours? ¿es suyo esto? [ess *s*ooyoh . . .]
  see **you**
youth hostel albergue juvenil [al-b*ai*r-gheh
  *h*ooveh-n*ee*l]
zero cero [th*e*h-roh]
  below zero bajo cero [b*a*h-*h*oh . . .]
zip una cremallera [kreh-ma-yeh-ra]
zona azul *restricted parking*

....

```
 0 cero [theh-roh]
 1 uno [oonoh]
 2 dos [doss]
 3 tres
 4 cuatro [kw–]
 5 cinco [theen-koh]
 6 seis [sayss]
 7 siete [see-eh-teh]
 8 ocho
 9 nueve [nweh-veh]
10 diez [dee-eth
11 once [on-theh]
12 doce [doh-theh]
13 trece [treh-theh]
14 catorce [kator-theh]
15 quince [keen-theh]
16 dieciseis [dee-ethee-sayss]
17 diecisiete [dee-ethee-see-eh-teh]
18 dieciocho [dee-ethee-ochoh]
19 diecinueve [dee-ethee-nweh-veh]
20 veinte [vain-teh]
21 veintiuno
22 veintidos
23 veintitres
24 veinticuatro
25 veinticinco
26 veintiseis
27 veintisiete
28 veintiocho
29 veintinueve
30 treinta [train-ta]
31 treinta y uno [traint-eye-oonoh]
40 cuarenta [kw–]
41 cuarenta y uno [kwarent-eye-oonoh]
50 cincuenta [theen-kwenta]
51 cincuenta y uno [theen-kwent-eye-oonoh]
60 sesenta
61 sesenta y uno [sessent-eye-oonoh]
70 setenta
```

71	setenta y uno [settent-eye-*oo*noh]
80	ochenta
81	ochenta y uno [ochent-eye-*oo*noh]
90	noventa
91	noventa y uno [novent-eye-*oo*noh]
100	cien [thee-*en*]
101	ciento uno
165	ciento sesenta y cinco [thee-*entoh*-sess*ent*-eye-th*ee*nkoh]
200	doscientos [doss-thee-*entoss*]
300	trescientos [tress-thee-*entoss*]
400	cuatrocientos [kwatroh-thee-*entoss*]
500	quinientos [keen-y*entoss*]
600	seiscientos [sayss-thee-*entoss*]
700	setecientos [seh-teh-thee-*entoss*]
800	ochocientos [otchoh-thee-*entoss*]
900	novecientos [noveh-thee-*entoss*]
1,000	mil [meel]
2,000	dos mil
4,653	cuatro mil seiscientos cincuenta y tres [kwatroh meel sayss-thee-*entoss* theen-kw*ent*-eye-tr*ess*]
1,000,000	un millón [meel-y*on*]

NB in Spain the comma is a decimal point; for thousands use a full-stop, eg 3.000

The alphabet: how to spell in Spanish
a [ah] *b* [beh] *c* [theh] *ch* [cheh] *d* [deh] *e* [eh]
f [eh-feh] *g* [heh] *h* [*a*tcheh] *i* [ee] *j* [hoh-ta]
k [ka] *l* [eh-leh] *ll* [eh-yeh] *m* [eh-meh] *n* [eh neh] *ñ* [en-yeh] *o* [oh] *p* [peh] *q* [koo] *r* [eh-reh]
rr [erreh] *s* [eh-seh] *t* [teh] *u* [oo] *v* [oo-veh]
w [oo-veh doh-bleh] *x* [eckeess] *y* [eegree-eh-ga]
z [theh-ta]